MY NIGERIA

MY NIGERIA

FIVE DECADES OF INDEPENDENCE

PETER CUNLIFFE-JONES

St. Martin's Press 🐟 New York

St. Martin's Griffin are registered trademarks in the United States, the
United Kingdom, Europe and other countries.

ISBN: 978-0-230-62023-0

Library of Congress Cataloging-in-Publication Data
Cunliffe-Jones, Peter.
    My Nigeria : five decades of independence / Peter Cunliffe-Jones.
       p.   cm.
    Includes bibliographical references and index.
    ISBN 978-0-230-62023-0 (hardback)
    1. Nigeria—History.   2. Nigeria—Politics and government.   3. Nigeria—
Social conditions.   4. Nigeria—Economic conditions.   5. Cunliffe-Jones,
Peter—Travel—Nigeria.   6. Nigeria—Description and travel.   I. Title.
DT515.57.C86   2010
966.9—dc22

                                                            2010007930

A catalogue record of the book is available from the British Library.

Design by Letra Libre, Inc.

First edition: September 2010

For
Nicola, Sam,
and
Nigerian friends

Contents

Acknowledgments

*F*ew books are the work of one man or woman alone. Writing this one, I have leaned heavily on the wisdom and friendship of many others. When I first moved to Nigeria, I was taught much about the country by my AFP news agency colleagues: Ade Obisesan, Aminu Abubakar, Joel Olatunde Agoi, Ola Awoniyi, Pius Utomi Ekpei, and Sam Audu, colleagues who became friends and still are. For four years, I worked with them and a small band of foreign journalists then based there: Barnaby Phillips and Dan Isaacs of the BBC, Glenn McKenzie of the Associated Press, Matthew Tostevin of Reuters, and William Wallis of the *Financial Times,* great reporters and companions all.

To write about Nigeria, I also depended on the ready willingness of Nigerians to talk about their hopes and fears, triumphs and disappointments. The journalist Gbenga Adefaye, the activist Clement Nwankwo, the priest and social critic Father Matthew Kukah, and the development consultant Paul Kalu in particular were generous with their time and ideas. Hassan Jimmoh drove me around Nigeria as safely as possible. And when I returned to the country a few years later, my friends Paul and Rex, and Valerie and Ayman Jammal were warmhearted hosts. All deserve my thanks.

I first thought of writing this book when I left Nigeria in 2003, but it took shape five years later, thanks, above all, to the encouragement of one other friend from Lagos, the American journalist and writer Stephan Faris. He urged me to write and offered invaluable advice when I did. He introduced me to my marvelous literary agent Elisabeth Weed and, through her, to my insightful editor Luba Ostashevsky, who took a manuscript and made it a book.

Above all, though, I owe a debt to my family. First, to my late grandparents, Hugo and Susan Marshall, who lent me their diaries, letters, and the memoirs of my great-great cousin, without which this book could not have been written. Second, I am indebted to my mother, Janet, my father, David, and my uncles Robert and David, who answered my questions with good grace and read and corrected the manuscript where it erred. Last, and above all, I owe thanks and a great debt of love to my wife, Nicola, whom I met in a restaurant off Awolowo Road in Lagos, for her patience and support, and to our son, Sam, whose sense of fun and easy laughter I much missed while working on this book over the past year.

They are all debts that I fully intend to honor.

Three Arrivals

"Why are you coming to Nigeria?" the immigration officer snapped, looking down at my passport. Her olive-green uniform was pulled tight around a solid frame. She tapped her pen on the counter impatiently. She was not smiling. It was 1998, and I was standing in line at the airport, waiting to have my papers stamped. Four years of living in Africa's most populous nation lay ahead of me, and I was nervous. The country was still under military rule. I hoped there'd be no last-minute hitch to stop me entering and taking up my post as the bureau chief of AFP, a Paris-based news wire. Perspiration broke out on my brow, and it was not from the heat.

"To work . . . I'm coming to work," I stuttered, pointing to my journalist's visa, hard-won a few days earlier at the embassy in Paris.

I had boarded the flight to Nigeria with a sense of trepidation. As a foreign correspondent, I was used to reporting from dangerous places. I had driven in and out of Sarajevo during the Bosnian war. I had canoed down the Ubangi River and hitchhiked across Zaire. I would later fly to Sierra Leone, and one day I would drive up the Khyber Pass to

Afghanistan. I would do all this quite happily, but Nigeria was different. I wasn't swooping in for a ten-day visit or reporting on events from a thousand miles away. I was coming to Nigeria to stay. And with me I was bringing the baggage of history: two bags, in fact, packed away in the hold.

The first contained a collection of letters home from a late nineteenth-century traveler, my great-grandmother's cousin, Edward Spenser Burns. He had worked for Belgium's King Leopold II in the Congo and would have done the same for Britain in Nigeria had he lived long enough to do so. The second contained the diaries of Sir Hugo Marshall, my grandfather. He had served as a colonial administrator in Nigeria for almost 30 years and had helped shape the constitution it had at independence in 1960.

 ∾

The first of us to arrive was my great-grandmother's cousin. It was December 5, 1883. The boat that had brought Edward to Africa, the *Corisco,* had sailed from Liverpool, a six-week trip down through the Bay of Biscay to the West African coast. Off Nigeria, it stopped at Bonny Island, then a major port of the Niger Delta, the great coastal expanse of rivers, creeks, and mangrove swamps where the mighty Niger River emerges into the sea.

On arrival at Bonny, the boat had been boarded by a plantation owner, a local chief and wealthy man. He had invited Edward and his companions to visit him and see one of his fields, some of the most productive in the palm oil business. Then the main commodity of trade with Europe, palm oil was used to make candles and grease for industrial machines. For a man new to Africa as my cousin was, a visit to a palm oil plantation was not an opportunity to miss.

The next morning, Edward climbed down the rough rope netting of his ship and clambered into the boat sent by the owner. He was the last aboard, and it was low in the water. The boat-master gave his orders. The crew of 36 was to take Edward and the rest of the party of 20 passengers to the plantation. The men nodded. Paddles dipped into the water and started to pull as the boat-master called the strokes. The men had to bend to the task. The tide was against them, and the work was hard. The passengers sat sheltered under a white awning, but the crew were out in the sun. They could not complain. They had no choice. The men doing the rowing were slaves.

Upstream, an hour later, the boat had to stop. The men could not pull any further. The tide was too low for the laden boat to pass. So passengers and crew got out. And from there, the party set off through the swampy terrain, the slaves wading a further half mile through water and mud, carrying Edward and his companions on their backs.

∾

Edward's encounter with Nigeria was brief. It came after failed attempts to carve out a career, first farming in New Zealand and Australia and then mining in Colorado. Back home and casting about for work, he had seen an advertisement offering employment with the International African Association (IAA), an ostensibly philanthropic body set up a few years earlier by King Leopold II to "explore Central Africa, eradicate slavery and civilize its people."[1] And, excited by the role that it offered, Edward joined up for three years' service. It would later become clear that the association was in fact an imperial enterprise, aimed at taking control of land across the Congo basin for the Belgian Crown.

The 1880s was the decade when Europe redrew Africa's borders, as governments and traders from across the old continent laid claim to

African land. Working for the association, Burns's job would be to acquire territory across the Congo, holding off French and Portuguese rivals and forcing "treaties" on local rulers that would see them cede sovereignty to his employers.

Edward's story tells how this happened—with men going from village to village, tricking or pressuring local leaders to give up their land, and exploiting them when they did so. It is the story of the plunder of Africa.

∿

Next to arrive in Nigeria was my grandfather, Sir Hugo Marshall. It was April 26, 1928. Since his cousin's brief sojourn in the country, much had changed. London had taken firm control of the territory that Burns had glimpsed on his short visit. In 1900 it had declared two protectorates, north and south, and then, in 1914, united them as one. The eradication of the sort of slavery witnessed by Burns—often used as justification for colonization—had been achieved at last. Trade had grown. And a new purpose had been found for empire in the meantime.

Unlike Burns, my grandfather had not come to Africa to seize land or claim a new colony. That had already been done. His was an age of government and progress, not of conquest and plunder, or that was how he saw it. Though it had begun in theft and bloodshed, the colonial mission in Nigeria was a noble one in his view, part of a wider effort by Europeans to bring peace, prosperity, and Western learning to a continent now almost entirely under European rule. It was work to which he was proud to put his name.

Hugo arrived in Africa almost straight out of university, aged 23, a young man as Burns had been. The day he arrived, after a three-week journey from England, a tropical storm struck the harbor, forcing him to stay aboard till it passed. But when finally ferried in across the breakers by skiff the next day, he found a world very different from that which Burns had seen when he had passed by nearly half a century earlier.

Besides a new harbor, Lagos now boasted broad roads and streetlights, a postal service, and a railway. Journeys inland were made using steam power, not slaves as packhorses. Off the boat, he was met by officials, completed immigration formalities, and took the night train to Osogbo, a few hours north of Lagos. From there, he went on to Akure, the up-country hill station where he would start work for the administration.

Starting out as a cadet officer, Hugo slowly climbed the ranks and built a career. He took court cases, oversaw road building, and checked tax receipts. He traveled often on field trips, mapping roads, carrying out research, and talking to Nigerians, asking what they sought from government. Having arrived in Nigeria before the Great Depression, he witnessed the painful effects it had on the colony, crippling Nigeria's nascent industries. Based during World War II in Ibadan, a large city an hour north of Lagos, he sought to defend the prices paid to farmers for their crops. The tariff proposed by British officials in Lagos one year was "exploitation," Hugo thundered, and he got things changed. As the war drew to a close, he drafted a plan to build roads, hospitals and schools, and to promote manufacturing and agriculture in the Western Region. It was part of a national postwar development drive. And once the war ended, he saw the colony's economy grow.

Working closely with the postwar government, my grandfather took part in crafting the first basic constitution, first working in 1947 in a tight circle of British officials, then five years later in a bigger group of British and Nigerian politicians. In 1952, he was named lieutenant governor for the Western Region and then chief secretary to the colony. When independence talks began, he left others to lay out the British position. He was instead often the negotiator between the Nigerian sides, cajoling them to work together. When the Yoruba leader Obafemi

Awolowo and the Igbo leader Nnamdi Azikiwe fell out, he shuttled between them, arranging meetings, holding dinners, and trying to get them to agree. As tensions between the rivals rose again one month, he invited them both to lunch, but this time the two would not come. Instead, they each served him with subpoenas, asking him to testify as a witness in cases they had filed against each other. And tensions between north and south were equally as great.

The constitution that emerged at the end was flawed. Those drafting it had good intentions, but it made Nigeria an unstable country. The colony became a federation built on three strong pillars—the governments of its northern, eastern, and western regions—but with little to cement them together as one nation. This was a mistake of historic proportions.

When finally he left Nigeria, on August 2, 1955, waving to a crowd of Nigerian and British friends, Hugo was both happy to leave and reluctant to go, fearful for what would happen when others left too. And he was right to be so. Within six short years of independence, the country fell apart. A coup took place that led to civil war. In the fighting, up to a million people died. Military rule followed, and in the decades that passed, the country suffered many years of bloodshed and misrule. In shaping the constitution used at independence, my grandfather had, I felt, helped create the conditions that led to this fall.

෴

Was that why I was there? I looked back at the woman behind the counter. She was still inspecting my passport, turning it slowly in her hand. She had spotted something, and I was worried. "You have been to Nigeria before," she said, looking at me after thumbing the pages for what seemed an inordinately long time. "It is true," I thought. "Not just me, but my family."

∾

I had decided I would come to Nigeria one day in late June 1986, as I stood in the cemetery of St. Nicholas's church in Winsley, a small village on a hill in southern England, half a mile from my grandparents' old home. The cemetery lies around the back of the church, down a short path from an arched wooden entrance gate, off to the right. My family had gathered there that warm June day to bury my grandfather and that was when I decided to go.

The call from my sister Judith telling me that my grandfather had died had come through the previous week on the last day of my second-year university exams. A few weeks earlier, I had made plans to visit my grandparents as soon as college was over for the year. At university, I had specialized in African history, and for my final-year paper I wanted to write a dissertation on the path Nigeria had taken to end colonial rule. My grandfather had agreed to help. With his death, I abandoned the idea, but not my plan to see Nigeria.

The following year, I finished my degree and, after working for 12 months to pay off student debts and raise some funds, I set off on a six-month trip across Africa. Nigeria was the halfway point. By December that year, I was stuck in a truck at a western border point, waiting to be allowed into the country. Up ahead, in the customs office, our driver was negotiating with the border guards. Our papers were all in order, but the guards wanted money, a *dash,* to let us through. It was 1988, and Nigeria was, even then, under army rule. Ibrahim Babangida was in power, and Sani Abacha was still to come.

The fees paid and our papers stamped, we entered the country and spent the first night camping on a beach near Lagos. We would not enter the city. It was too dangerous, we were told. Most of those on the trip did not want to spend much time in Nigeria anyway. It was a troubled place, and they wanted to get in and get out quickly. This was under-standable given the country's reputation. My first visit lasted four days.

After staying on the beach outside Lagos, we spent a night at Benin and Calabar. I swam by a waterfall in Cross River State, a beautiful spot on the border Nigeria shared with Cameroon. And then we drove north to a border crossing and were gone. Three months later, I reached jour-ney's end in Kenya. Some carried on, but I had run out of money. I bought an air ticket home, spent my last few coins in a restaurant in Nairobi, and took a flight for England.

A few weeks after I returned, I went to visit my grandmother, Susan. She got out some of my grandfather's old letters and diaries from a cup-board in the attic and gave me them to read. "Nigeria is troubled now, but your grandfather was optimistic this would change," she told me. "You should go there again," she said.

As my grandmother started preparing dinner, I left the house. Alone, I walked up the hill that led back up to the church at the top. I entered the cemetery and stood there before my grandfather's grave. It was the first time I had been there in two years, the first time since he had died. Standing there, I read the inscription etched on his gravestone.

In Loving Memory of

Hugo Frank Marshall

Born Limpley Stoke 1905
Died Murhill 1986

Nigerian Administration
1928–1955

All Manner of Thing Shall Be Well

❦

I looked back at the woman behind the counter. "Yes," I told her. I had visited the country before. I had visited briefly, almost a decade earlier, as a tourist. I had traveled on a truck across the continent when I was twenty-three. I had enjoyed my stay in Nigeria, brief though it had been. And I hoped that would not stop me from returning now.

A smile spread across the woman's face. It was the first time that day that she had had someone entering as a tourist, or someone who had done so in the past. "Normally it is only business here. Money. You have been here before as a tourist and you enjoyed it," she said. And smiling broadly, she stamped my passport and handed it back.

"You are welcome to Nigeria," she said.

Whatever lay ahead of me, I was about to find out.

CHAPTER 1

A Place of Great Potential

L *agos is black Africa's* megacity. Located six degrees north of the equator on the country's south-facing Atlantic coast, it has a climate that is hot and humid the whole year round. Home today to more than 15 million people, the country's hustling, bustling, trading capital is noisy and violent and pulses with life. From the tall towers of its waterfront districts to the low-rise slums that are home to millions, it hums with activity, with people making deals, making money, taking a chance, and getting by.

In skyscraper offices on Lagos Island and around a groaning port, its bankers and oilmen—enjoying the wealth generated by a multibillion-dollar oil industry—make trades worth tens of millions of dollars every day. It is home to insurance and shipping firms that play the markets worldwide. And on its streets, thousands of high-stakes battles take place each night as the poor fight to survive. A combustible place, it can explode into violence at a moment's notice. A vast city, it is congested and grinds into gridlock twice a day.

Like Mumbai, the home of Bollywood romances, Lagos seems as much a product as a producer of its thriving film business. Every year, Nollywood, the Nigerian Bollywood, tells extraordinary tales of life and death, money, and sex in hundreds of full-length features released on DVD and video. But to residents of Lagos, its films are not pointless make-believe. In the city's rabbit-warren slums, such as Mushin and Oshodi, the streets are packed with people stepping between broken-down cars, open sewers, and run-down buildings. Those who live there have lost out, but cling on, like survivors in a storm, to their Lagos dreams. Slumdogs they may be. But like the slumdogs of Mumbai, they see hope around the corner and a reason to stay.

A few miles away live those who have made it—the foreigners, the oilmen, the politicians, and the bureaucrats. Their Lagos—the one I came to live in—is quite different, a place of fancy flats and spacious villas, broad streets, lush gardens with bougainvilleas and palm trees, a polo club, a yacht club, restaurants, and nightclubs, where beggars line the streets outside, dodging the expensive cars and trucks, while night-girls dance for free and offer sex at five dollars a time.

For those who have made it, life is good. They have to suffer the pollution and the traffic jams, the power cuts, and the threat of crime. But they are rich and they are free. And to the poor, they are tantalizingly close: The rich—the people most at fault for running Nigeria into the ground since independence—are not people to blame, but to envy, people to emulate if only one is able.

And Lagos, my Lagos, the city where I came to live in 1998, is this clash of these two worlds: a permanent collision of humbling wealth and staggering poverty, soaring hope and frustrated ambition, frightening chaos and unruly order; a city always on the edge of mayhem and always offering the hungry a last chance, a hope, a dream of success.

❧

The original name for Lagos, the island that lies at the heart of the city, was Eko, an old Nigerian word for a battleground or war camp. The island was a settlement and this gave the place its name. But when Portuguese sailors sailed up the coast in the fifteenth century, they saw something else: not the island, but the lagoon behind it and the safe harbor it offered. They named it Lagos—from the Portuguese for lagoon or lake—and to the world over, Lagos has been its name ever since.

After its settlement, and after discovery by the Portuguese, came slave traders who made the island a home to the slave trade for centuries. For hundreds of years, they traded from camps on its marshy shores. And then, from the 1850s onward, it became home to the British, who came to stop the slave trade at its source. Today it is again a pure Nigerian city: vast, unruly, exhausting, and compelling.

From the port the white men built, the city erupts outward, an explosion of concrete, cars, and construction heading 30 miles north and inland from the sea. The packed mainland districts, a mix of towers and low-rise buildings, are cut through by trunk roads and highways that every day carry thousands of cars and buses taking people to and from the business districts located on the islands near the shore. Between the city and the sea lies a peninsula that shelters the lagoon, serves as a battered breakwater, and holds back the Atlantic tide.

The Atlantic is not the only tide that threatens Lagos. With a growing population, today more than 15 million, eating, defecating, buying, and throwing away, it is unsurprising its government has never yet mastered the awesome task of keeping it neat, ordered, and clean. Instead, tons of waste, human and industrial, lie every day by the roadside or seep into streams leading to the inland shore. Certainly, today, the authorities are making an effort, but when they do they are often overwhelmed.

The city is noisy and polluted. The power grid rarely works, so the fumes of tens of thousands of generators supplying power to homes and offices pollute the air, making it heavy and difficult to breathe. And it is dangerous. Mangled cars lie at the roadside and, on occasion, mangled bodies too, the victim of an accident or a murder, or just a hapless natural death. Sometimes, nobody knows. When a senior policeman went missing one month, the police searched the waters under a bridge for his corpse. When six hours had passed, they stopped looking after turning up 23 bodies, none of them the one they were seeking. A few weeks later, I went sailing, and my dinghy capsized. As I surfaced spluttering, a corpse floated past a few feet away. I shuddered in the water and climbed back aboard.

To skirt the city's most congested districts, the authorities in the 1970s built a looping, eight-mile-long highway on pillars known as the Third Mainland Bridge. It runs through the lagoon, north to south, and ends in the islands. Though the traffic is normally fender-to-fender, there are so many cars on the packed mainland roads that the bridge is still the fastest way in. From the shores of Ikeja, on the mainland, it runs south past shantytowns built on stilts, cuts through the smoke rising from saw mills at the water's edge, passes the tall towers of Lagos Island, owned by banks and shipping and oil companies, and drops down past the port—full of boats, buildings, containers, and cranes—to enter the sanctuary of the islands.

Like most who could—the foreigners, oilmen, bankers, and politicians—I made my home on one of the islands: Ikoyi. It sits opposite Victoria Island, the tip of the peninsula, and next to Lagos Island itself, the original heart of the city. Once, it was a smart district. On the walls of my house, a two-story place built in the 1970s and surrounded by palm trees and flowers, pictures taken when my grandfather lived and worked in Lagos in the 1950s show broad roads and elegant, shaded sidewalks. By the time I arrived, half a century later, Ikoyi's roads were potholed and lacked proper pavement or street lighting. Walking home late at night from one of its still-thriving bars and restaurants, dodging the police and the robbers, I had to step carefully to avoid tripping on garbage, slipping on human and animal waste, and landing in a fetid gutter.

But even for those living in luxury, paying rents and property prices among the highest in the world, Lagos is a dangerous place to live. I might go on the weekend to dance at nightclubs in Yaba or Ikeja on the mainland. But if I did, I would go in daylight and stay there till dawn. Every day the newspapers were full of crime stories. Armed robbers attack people in the streets and in their homes. Travel after dark is considered unsafe.

One night soon after I arrived, I was heading to the airport later than planned for a trip overseas. Coming off the Third Mainland Bridge into Ikeja, I asked Hassan, my driver, to take a shortcut through Oshodi, one of the roughest neighborhoods. This was a mistake. As we crossed the bridge over Oshodi market, we got stuck in a traffic jam. The cars in front soon cleared, and we set off again. But a few yards farther on the car stalled. Our lights went out, and the streetlights weren't working.

Hassan got out and raised the hood. I followed. This was my second mistake. A lookout saw me and, within moments, a gang had pounced. Four armed men surrounded us demanding money. I did not have much on me. "You can have everything but it is not much," I said. Their leader pushed me back against the car and put his gun to my head and a knife to my throat.

I got into the car to look for money. As I did, Hassan overheard the robbers arguing. They couldn't agree what to do. Two wanted to kill us and take whatever we had—the car, my bags, and my money. The others wanted to let us go. Killing a foreigner would bring too much trouble. The police knew their names and would come after them. It was not worth the risk, they said.

Thinking quickly, Hassan assured the men that I did have money. He would get in and hand it over. But first he would restart the car, though with the hood still up, so we could drive off once they let us. Stupidly, they agreed. The engine running, he lifted the hand brake and hit the gas. No money had changed hands, but off we went, bumping over one robber, hitting a second with my door, and knocking the others sideways. The hood flapping wildly against the windshield, we drove away blind. As bullets hit the sides of the car, I peered out of my window to see and scream directions to Hassan: "Go right! Go left! Don't hit that wall!" Eventually, the shooting stopped. We slowed the car, lowered the hood, and resumed our journey.

I felt shattered, but I breathed again. We had gotten away.

That was Lagos. Every night, before I slept, I always made a tour of my house, checking the windows, pulling down the metal shutters, locking myself in, and listening. Often the sounds I heard were of gunfire.

∾

The city is chaos and mayhem. And yet, despite all its problems, there is more to Lagos than that, more to it than paupers and gangsters, bankers and politicians, Nollywood and Lagos rap. There are beautiful places, a richness of culture, a depth of color, and resilient people. It is a great place to live and to watch people work on their dreams.

One morning, I headed out on assignment, crossing the bridge to the mainland once more and turning onto a freeway. It was a grim spot I had passed many times. But as we drove, I saw a small strip of land just off the road, perhaps half an acre in size, one I hadn't noticed before. Fenced off from the freeway and a line of wrecked cars and buses was a garden.

It was not just any garden, but, in a city known for its squalor, a garden with a mission. The ambitious title stenciled on its signboard read "Project for the Beautification of Lagos."

I stopped the car and drove back. "Good morning," I said, walking toward the gate and the man I had spotted emerging from a garden hut. I told him I was a journalist and asked about the project. Was this all his own work? He pointed to the name of the church sponsoring the initiative. They funded it, and he did the work. He was retired now, so he had the time.

"This is not my job. This is what I do for love. Lagos is not beautiful yet. But this is a place with great potential."

I asked about the flowers he was growing. Scribbling notes, I marveled at what he had achieved already in poor soil surrounded by roadside wreckage: great bursts of color; lilies and orchids; ferns and miniature palms; verdant grasses and fronds; brilliant red, yellow, and orange flowers; petals in subtle shades of lilac and purple. The beautification of Lagos is one hell of a project, I thought. But at least someone was trying.

ॐ

The day I met that gardener, almost four decades had passed since the country became self-governing. The constitution crafted by my grandfather and others in the 1950s had failed the country. Of those four decades since independence, the army had been in power for nearly three. Ever since independence in 1960, Nigerian leaders had promised progress. What they had delivered was six coups, a bloody civil war, and a stuttering economy. When oil prices boomed in the 1970s, the army spent freely on big projects. But ordinary Nigerians had had little to show for it. In the 1980s, there was a brief return to a civilian regime, a four-year hiatus in army rule. It was followed by a consumer boom, a bust, the return of the soldiers, and a new series of economic plans. More coups took place. Each new leader promised progress that each failed to deliver. By the time I arrived in 1998, life for most was hard and precarious. Too few people had regular jobs. Real incomes had fallen by a third since independence. People struggled to work, live, and feed their families. Life expectancy, as measured at birth, was only 45 years.

But the month I flew in was a time of new hope. Just two weeks earlier, the dictator Sani Abacha had died. Abacha was the army chief who seized power in 1993 a few months after his predecessor quit office. For half a decade, Abacha had subjected opponents to jail or assassination while he stole billions from the public coffers and ran down the economy. When he died from a reported heart attack, there were celebrations. But there were still no rules for handing over power. The army had suspended the constitution when it last seized control.

With Abacha gone, the new man in charge was Abdulsalami Abubakar, a slow-talking man with a hangdog expression. Though almost unknown to the public, he had been Abacha's number two. Now he was in charge of Nigeria, and no one knew his plans. A month later, riots erupted when the country's leading opposition figure, Moshood Abiola, died in jail.

The next day, Abubakar moved. He announced a series of elections to end army rule and hand power to civilians. Unlike his predecessors, he kept his promises. Politicians who had been sent into hiding or prison hurriedly reemerged, and three political parties were formed. The first elections took place in December 1998. And by the time the main voting occurred two months later, the poll came down to a contest between two men, both flawed.

One was Olu Falae, a soon-to-be-forgotten former finance minister. He represented the Alliance for Democracy, a group of southern politicians who had opposed Abacha and had little support in the north. The other was a former general, Olusegun Obasanjo. His Peoples Democratic

Party (PDP) was more of a mixed bag. Some had bravely stood up against Abacha—Obasanjo himself had been jailed—but others had a less honorable record. But, mixed bag or no, Obasanjo's party had a stronger national network than its rivals and a clearer idea of Nigerian politics. "Elections first. Policies will come later," a PDP spokesman told me when I asked what the party stood for. "The first step is to take power."

∾

With the departure of the soldiers expected, the elections of February 1999 were a time of new hope for Nigeria. They were the first elections in 20 years that would result in a change in power. What the voters wanted above all was clear. They wanted the soldiers to leave, and they wanted change. The problem was that neither voters nor candidates had spelled out what else they meant by change.

"Ah! This Nigeria," Remi Adeyinka, a market trader, harrumphed, shaking her head as she queued at a makeshift polling station near my home on polling day. ID papers in hand, she adjusted the wrapper she wore round her waist as both skirt and sign of her political allegiance. The face on the wrapper was that of Falae. What did she want from the election? I asked. She shifted on her feet. "It is time for these soldier boys to go. They have ruined this country for too long. Now it is time for change," she said.

Mama Bella Afolabe, Mrs. Adeyinka's neighbor in the line, nodded in agreement. "These men with their uniforms, their guns, they have done nothing for us. Our new president, he will change Nigeria. He must change Nigeria. I hope so." She supported Obasanjo.

But what change? The people had not decided who would run in the election. The military had. They had picked the parties and the candidates. And the people whom the military allowed to run had not said how they would govern once in power. So what change would Nigeria see? No one knew. With the backing of the PDP machine, Obasanjo walked the election, winning by 18 million votes to 11 million. He had clear national support, but he had never declared his policies.

~

In his inauguration speech in the capital, Abuja, three months later, the new president, who had led the country before in the 1970s, sounded pained by the state he found it in today. "Nigerians are hurting," he said. The country, so rich in talent and resources, home to great writers and artists, businessmen and entrepreneurs, and rich in land and minerals, had been crippled by years of misrule. It would be so no longer, he pledged. There would be neither sacred cows, nor no-go areas in the fight against corruption and abuse of power. He would bring change, the old soldier told the audience standing in the square, listening on radio, and watching on TV. And, for a while, a few believed him.

In his first hundred days, the new president reined in spending and promised money for health and education. He reshuffled the military, sacked those who had staged coups or held political posts in the past, and sent an anticorruption bill to parliament. I wrote an article for the *Economist* titled "Nigeria's New Broom," to highlight the sweeping changes.[1]

Over the next four years, government finances indeed improved, bolstered not only by the rising price of oil and gas but also by economic reforms. Corruption was far from eradicated, but outright theft from the public purse was reduced. The country, for years an international pariah, subject to sanctions, was readmitted to the world stage. Life became a little freer for political activists and campaigners. There was an important change for ordinary people. Cell phones, once banned by the military, were approved, and their use became widespread—within months, it seemed that everyone, from taxi drivers to market traders, was talking nonstop.

All this was good. But it was not enough. With the army off the streets, violence erupted. Though direct theft had dropped, corruption continued to eat into the public purse, and vast sums were wasted. Money promised for schools and clinics was not disbursed. A new national stadium was built, costing more than a year's combined budget for health and education, though Nigeria already had eight stadiums and few thought a new one was needed. The electricity network remained weak and erratic and most people were still not connected to it at all. At my home, I had power for two to three hours a day.

Progress that Nigerians could measure in the safety of their streets, in growth in jobs, in the money in their pockets, and in the care given in clinics and schools did not come. Instead, inflation rose, army abuses continued, and life remained hard for most. In trips around the country, I saw the same grinding poverty persist.

Johnson Afolabi's story was a typical one of people falling through the cracks. Aged 14 when I met him, he was 7 when his mother passed away and 12 when his father was shot dead by police at a checkpoint for failing to pay them a kickback to let him through.

Johnson left school and became an apprentice electrician. The job paid something, but not enough. For a while, he and his siblings lived with relatives and they could get by. But the house was overcrowded, and the families fell out. They moved to Makoko, a slum district of wooden huts built on stilts out over the fetid waters of Lagos lagoon.

Desperate for money, Johnson took to petty thieving. He had skills as an electrician but not as a thief. He was soon arrested, and it was after he was caught that I met him, lolling at a police station I was visiting, unable to pay bail and worried about his brother and sisters, who had no one to look after them. With no education, no proper home, and no prospects of work, the outlook for him, and them, looked bleak indeed.

To me, this was Nigeria, the country birthed by my grandfather. Johnson was a bright young man and not a bad one. But the system had failed him. "What do I do?" he asked me. "I no get education. I no get father, mother. I no get proper job. What do I do?" With all its wealth—the riches brought by oil—and human resources, Nigeria should have been a good home to a young man like Johnson. But decades after independence, it wasn't. What was the reason? I had no answer to the question, just as I had no answer for Johnson Afolabi. Over the next four years, I set out to get one.

CHAPTER 2

The Troubles of Nigeria

*T*he problems I saw in those first few months were not limited to Lagos. The daily clashing of Nigeria's two worlds—the steepening wealth and staggering poverty, the frightening chaos and unruly order—were part of life all around the country. The problems were not new. But they were getting worse. And I wanted to know why.

In 1958, two years before independence, a literary talent emerged in Nigeria that lit the world stage. *Things Fall Apart* was one of the first great African novels. Many other literary works followed from the writer Chinua Achebe. Then, in 1983, Achebe added a political polemic to his list, a booklet called *The Trouble with Nigeria*. Honest and thoughtful, it offered an unflinching look at Nigeria's problems and an indictment of the country's rulers.

After almost a decade spent out of the country receiving medical treatment for a back injury, Achebe returned to Nigeria on a brief visit home in 1999, and I went to meet him at his home in the east. The writer was alarmed by the depths to which his country had sunk.

"Nigeria is a country in crisis," Achebe said. In the years he had been away, little had changed for the better. In fact, things had gotten worse. "Nigeria is a house that has fallen. The level of crime in Lagos, the social collapse, the trouble we have here in Onitsha are all part of it. This house has fallen," he said.

Arriving at Lagos, Achebe had been disconcerted by the number of unemployed young men he saw hanging around at the airport. They were hoodlums, he said. "What are they doing? Why aren't they working?" And he'd been shocked to be told, by the city police chief, that he shouldn't drive home at night. "He said it would be too dangerous," the writer recalled, still astonished at the thought. "When I was a young man, the only thing that worried us, driving at night, was being hit by lumber lorries without their lights on. Not highwaymen. Not armed robbers."

It was important to know why this was still happening, Achebe told me. When he wrote his polemic in 1983, he'd explained the reason for Nigeria's malaise. "The trouble with Nigeria is simply and squarely a failure of leadership," the author famously declared. There is nothing basically wrong with Nigerian character, he said. There was nothing wrong either with Nigerian land, or the climate, or anything else. "The Nigerian problem is the unwillingness or inability of its leaders to rise to the responsibility, to the challenge of personal example which are the hallmarks of true leadership."[1]

Was that still the case? I asked. It was. "If poor leadership was the cause of the problem then, it is still the case today," Achebe said.

∞

The first duty of any government, the first test of a country's leader, is to protect its people from harm. But would the new government live up to its duty to safeguard the Nigerian people?

From the day Obasanjo took office, trouble erupted. Starting in the delta town of Warri, disturbances and street battles broke out around the country. Week after week and month after month, towns and villages broke out into fighting. Some battles were gang wars fought for control of the streets and the crime operations that they ran there. Others were battles staged by politicians to whip up support among people divided along ethnic or religious lines. Others were spontaneous clashes over land and resources. But, whatever the cause, time after time, the government, police, and army failed to stop the killing; innocents dying with the guilty.

Estimates of the death toll varied. The government said that the unrest killed 10,000 in the first four years of Obasanjo's rule. This was more than the total number of dead in two decades in the Middle East, the violence that dominates world news headlines. But even this was an underestimate. The real toll was at least twice that number, one security official told me. And from what I could see, the government was doing little to stop it.

From village courtyard to city center, I witnessed killings go unchecked. Fighting broke out one week in Sagamu, a town a few miles northeast of Lagos. It was a small town, and the trouble would have been easy to stop. Word had got around that a Hausa woman had shown disrespect at a Yoruba festival. This was a serious matter. Outraged Yoruba youths had killed the woman. The next day, the Hausas retaliated. Calls went out to surrounding towns to bring in some weapons. Outnumbered, the small police contingent panicked and withdrew. And when they left, a battle erupted.

I drove there that afternoon with two colleagues. The road in was all but deserted. Roadside shacks were barricaded up. We pulled up at a police roadblock on the outskirts of town. A policeman told us we could enter. We went in on foot and, at first, the fighting appeared over. But then, as we turned a corner and neared the center, we could hear shouts and cries that told us what was happening.

Up ahead, we saw two lines drawn up across a wasteland. As we stood there, I spotted a group of Hausa youths a few yards back from the rest. They had captured a young Yoruba man and had hacked him half to death. Across the town's new front line, the Yoruba had captured a Hausa boy. The Yoruba youth was still alive and suffering. One eye was bloodied. The other had spilled on his cheek. He tried to cry out, but no words came. The young men around him were taking turns to heat their blades in a fire and poke and twist them in his wounds. Their rivals across the way were doing the same to the boy they had captured.

The group nearest me gathered around and started hacking at the boy. With a final chop, his head lolled back. He was dead. I had done nothing to help him. I couldn't. I turned, blinking, and was sick.

Achebe was right. Nigerians are not predisposed to fighting. Violence is not bred in at birth. It is not preset in Nigerian character. But from Lagos to Kaduna, Kano to Sagamu, the fighting was killing hundreds, sometimes thousands. And the problem was the leaders who stirred the fighting, even ran the gangs, and did not care when a hundred people died. The failure was a failure of leadership. I saw it right across Nigeria.

~

Traveling the roads of Nigeria for four years, from the lush green hills of the south to the dust-dry plains of the north, it might have seemed to be a poor country. It might have appeared to be a place of rundown homes and closed factories, of poor farmers in fields and peasants around an empty well. With more people living on a dollar a day than anywhere save India and China, it is doubtless a country of the poor. But a poor country it is not. There is money in Nigeria from oil and gas, money enough to make many people rich, as I saw in Ikoyi, in Lagos bars and restaurants, in flashy cars, and in fancy yachts.

One year, I went to see the home of one of the wealthiest families. Mai Deribe, one of the richest traders in the north, had died a few months earlier in a hospital in Saudi Arabia. Born to a modest family of northeastern cattle traders, he had used his trading contacts and business skills to build an empire in government supplies and oil sales. It had made him a very wealthy man, and I wanted to see what he'd done with it.

Maiduguri, a city as far northeast as it is possible to go in Nigeria, was Deribe's hometown. On an average day, the city is quiet and calm, its white-walled streets hum with the activities of any small country town, punctuated five times daily by the calls of the muezzin and the gentle noise of crickets chirping in the heat.

I had arranged my visit months beforehand, hoping to meet the tycoon, take a look at his business empire, and see his family home. When he passed away, I shelved my plans to visit. But a few weeks later, I received an unexpected call inviting me to come up to be shown around by one of the late man's sons.

The drive to Maiduguri took many hours. I flew first to Abuja, then headed north. I was tired when I finally got there. The next day, Deribe's son Ibrahim picked me up early from my hotel and drove me out to his family seat. We passed the city center, turned a corner, and there it was: a mansion behind high walls. We approached and entered through tall iron gates. We parked our car and went up to the house. At the entrance was a welcome mat. When I stepped on it, the mat vibrated gently to brush away the dust from my feet. Ibrahim opened the door and we went inside.

Deribe had, at one time, been the treasurer of the ruling party, and one of his daughters was married to the *shehu* of Borno, a powerful traditional leader. In the entryway were photographs of almost every past president and military ruler. In the hall, a guest book recorded the names of those who had come to pay their respects when he passed away. It was a roll call of the national elite.

The home we were visiting took eight years to construct. It had cost Deribe $100 million. Aping the kings of France, who sparked a revolution with their follies, he had called it the Nigerian Versailles, and grandiose it certainly was.

"This is the main hall," Ibrahim said, waving his arm down a 200-meter passage lined with Italian marble and satin curtains. On one side was a huge meeting room with a carved wooden table. On the other was a vast dining room with seats for 20 people. At the far end, past more rooms and a staircase, was a room called the Gold Room. "You'll see why inside," Ibrahim said. I pushed the door and went in. I was stunned; surrounded by a more ostentatious display of wealth than I had ever seen. Thick bars of solid gold ran in columns up the walls. Gold nuggets in the carpet spelled out Deribe's name in Arabic lettering. Solid gold chairs were placed at the four corners. A gold chandelier hung overhead.

We went upstairs, past diamond-tipped chandeliers, to more rooms, a splendid master bedroom, and en suite bathrooms complete with gold taps. How many rooms were there up there? I did not know. I'd lost count. And then, after half an hour, I'd seen it all. Ibrahim led me to the exit. We stepped out of the house and entered an empty courtyard. Beyond its high walls, I could hear the sound of insects in the grass and then, strangely, nothing. No cars were driving past. No factories were humming in the distance. There was virtual silence from the town.

I was uneasy asking the question that jumped out at me. The money had come from trading in oil and supplies. It had not come from industry or farming, businesses that create jobs and income. It had come not from making things but from selling oil, a business that benefits only the few in Nigeria.

"Did your father do anything here with his money, beyond building this house? Did he set up any businesses here?" I asked Ibrahim. Borno, home to Maiduguri, is the poorest state in Nigeria.

Ibrahim thought for a moment and then took me across the road to a simple mosque and school Deribe had built for the city. There was more he had done, but not much, it appeared. The contrast with the marble-lined palace, its chandeliers, and the Gold Room could not have been greater.

As I said goodbye and turned to go, a boy sitting in the shade of a nearby tree spotted me. Though crippled by polio, he grabbed the hand of the blind old man sitting beside him and led him over to me, bowl in hand, asking for charity. That was the problem. Oil wealth does not trickle down.

∽

After the president and the businessmen, the most powerful people in Nigeria are the country's 36 state governors, chief power brokers in the three dozen states of the federation. What would they do to improve the people's lives?

I set off one day from Abuja to Gusau, the capital of Zamfara State, to meet a governor and see his example. Zamfara is a poor state and its people complain of misrule and corruption. The drive there took many hours along deteriorating roads. Camels grazed under baobab trees as we passed. A group of Fulani herdsmen sat by a pool with their long-horned cattle. It was a beautiful scene, but the place was hurting. I was visiting Gusau for good reason. A year earlier, in the elections of 1999, a former bank official called Ahmed Sani had won the governorship by promising *shariah* law, government by Islamic rules overseen by Islamic courts. Was this an answer to the troubles of Nigeria?

Portrayed in the West as a charter for extremists—sanctioning the stoning of adulterers and flogging of penitents—the shariah is more complex than that. It is the set of law codes and practices at the heart of Islam, laying out Muslims' social and religious rights and duties. Under Islamic law, alcohol is banned, the mixing of men and women is regulated, and, in conservative countries, people may be flogged or even stoned for "crimes" such as sex outside marriage. These measures are, however, only a small part of what the shariah means to most Muslims. To the great majority, it simply means God's law: just and compassionate. It brings Islam to its rightful place in the heart of government. It orders alms-giving from rich to poor. And it demands honesty from officials high and low in government.

To understand the appeal, I attended a pro-shariah gathering in the town. The introduction of the code had been criticized by Christians in the north, I told Abdullah Ibrahim, a doctor I met in the crowd. Why did Muslims need the shariah?

I expected a lesson on religion. What I got was politics. "Our soldiers and politicians are all thieves," said the doctor. "They have been since the start, in 1960." With the shariah as law, religious courts could act to stop abuse and theft, the doctor told me. They could act in a way the state courts never would. Government by God's law would be just and fair to all. "Without the shariah in the north, I see no hope for us in Nigeria," he said.

❧

Ahmed Sani, the man who had introduced the code to Zamfara, smiled when I told him the story. "You see," he said. "Nothing to fear." CNN was on the television in the background. Sani himself was as welcoming as he could be, reaching out to pump my hand and ask about my journey.

He had put on a little weight since he had become governor, I told him, judging by photos from before the campaign. He laughed. "It is a common thing among politicians," he said. "One of the hazards of office." But Sani had more than weight gain in common with traditional politicians, more than he wanted his supporters to believe. The idea to run for governor on the "shariah ticket" had not been born of religious conviction. It was political. There were better-known politicians who had vied for the position of Zamfara governor but Sani's adoption of the shariah platform won him his supporters. While he espoused the cause, he was not sincere.

In February 2000, the questions most widely posed about the shariah concerned the rights of women and the Christian minority. Sani assured me that nothing dreadful would happen to anyone. He was wrong. In 2001, a 35-year-old divorced woman called Safiya Husseini, from a village near Sokoto, appeared before a court just north of Gusau. The fifth of 12 children of a peasant farming family, Safiya had grown up illiterate in her remote village, a hardworking girl known for helping her family on their farm. Married off at 12, then divorced, she had been unmarried when she got pregnant by a 60-year-old neighbor who had promised her marriage but reneged on his commitment. A few months after her child was born, she was reported to an Islamic court for sex outside marriage. And, found guilty, she was sentenced to death by stoning. The man involved was released without charge.

The case against Safiya, and the sentence that followed, outraged many Christians in Nigeria and millions more around the world. The government intervened, and her conviction was overturned. Three other cases followed suit, all revealing an injustice at the heart of the system.

Although these cases made world headlines, they were not what most interested most Nigerians. What did was corruption. And it was clear from the start that this would be the greatest test of the shariah in Zamfara.

As a lifelong public servant, Governor Sani's official salary, earned at the Central Bank and then as governor, was clearly too low to explain his luxurious lifestyle: nine houses, seven farms, and other assets. Some of his wealth had been acquired when he worked at the Central Bank, in charge of funds for peacekeeping operations in Liberia, he admitted. "When I was at the Central Bank, in the foreign exchange, I would take $800,000 to the Villa [the seat of the presidency]," he told me. Once there, "sometimes the officer would dash me $10,000 or $5,000," he said. With weekly or monthly trips to the Villa, such bribes, and others he admitted to, could easily build into a fortune. So would he give the money back? Would he crack down on corruption?

Sani looked uncomfortable. He knew that taking public money was wrong and would not do it now, he said. It was against the shariah. But things had been different then. What had happened before was an old story. And besides, he was allowing friends and relatives to stay in some of his homes.

"The important thing is that the courts are now Islamic courts. They can do as they wish. The courts can act if they see corruption at any level of government. I won election as a good Muslim. And a good Muslim I am. It is for Allah to punish me if I sin," he declared.[2]

Was it true? I returned to Zamfara three years later and found Abdullah, the pro-shariah doctor I had met a few months after the law code came into effect. The change that people had wanted in the north—Islamic courts ensuring just rule and an end to corruption—had not come, he told me. Nobody powerful had been brought to book for corruption or theft. People had died for the shariah. Protests by Christians in Kaduna, another northern city, had led to thousands of deaths. But the government had not improved.

Why? I asked. Abdullah was silent for a moment. As a Muslim, he still welcomed the shariah, he said. But he was disillusioned with the governor. Working in public health, he had seen little good come from the change. There had been no more money for hospitals or clinics since the shariah was introduced; no more money for doctors or nurses. "Our leaders are not sincere. They are just thieves. This is not the shariah," he said. Who did he blame? "Ahmed Sani," he said, showing me a newspaper report of corruption allegations against the governor.

"People hoped the shariah would bring us justice," the doctor told me. "But what have we got? The same politicians as before and nothing else has changed. We have the appearance of Islamic law but not the real thing. They are fakes, the lot of them. It did not bring change."

∾

Radical ideas were not restricted to the north. As army rule ended, a crime wave erupted in major cities, as well as unrest. By 2001, crime had turned Onitsha, the biggest trading city in the east, into a place where gunshots rang out all day. Home to half a million people on the eastern bank of the Niger, the city was virtually lawless. Its residents were so afraid of being robbed or killed that they applauded when the state governor of Anambra, Chinwoke Mbadinuju, brought in vigilantes to fight crime.

To see what was happening, I drove to Onitsha. At a bridge across the Niger, I looked over and wondered whether the vigilantes would be easy to meet. Like the shariah's proponents, they had a fearsome reputation. Was it justified? Were they the answer to chaos and crime in Nigeria?

I first went to the governor's mansion in the state capital, Awka. From there, I was directed to a dingy three-story building known as the White House in the heart of the Onitsha market. As I climbed a dank stairwell that led up through the building, I got a first glimpse of the vigilantes' methods. In an unlit room off the staircase, I saw a group of vigilantes with ten men they had arrested. The detainees were kneeling on the floor. They had been beaten. Some were bleeding from the face, others from the body.

Hustled upstairs by a guard, I was taken to see Monday Okorie, the group's commander for this district. Okorie was lounging back in an office chair well past its prime, its foam padding bursting out of its black plastic covering. A bottle of gin lay half drunk on the table next to two guns. A bodyguard lay on a sofa nearby, holding a machete with one hand and scratching his crotch with the other. A juju monkey skull hung from the doorway.

The vigilantes were not supposed to detain people, I told Okorie. By law, the vigilantes were supposed to detain suspects and hand them straight over to the police. His men were beating up the suspects held downstairs. There were widespread reports that they killed the people who confessed under torture. This was not progress for Nigeria.

"We do not kill and we do not harm. We just arrest criminals and give them to the police," Okorie said.

"This is not what is happening downstairs," I replied.

"You don't know what you saw," Okorie replied.

"What did I see?" I asked.

"You saw us clearing vermin from the streets," he told me.

Outside, in the market, the traders told me they had welcomed the vigilantes at first. They had thanked the governor. But now the Bakassis, as the vigilantes were known, were becoming a problem. Little more than thugs themselves, they were abusing the powers the governor had given them, extorting money from stallholders and abusing young girls. The Bakassis were being used by the governor to harass and kill opponents. The Bakassis had become part of the problem: killers and thieves.

∾

If the government, the businessmen, and the governors were not helping
the people, then who would? Would a band of rebels? Shortly after I arrived in Nigeria, I drove south to the Niger Delta, the place where
Africa's third-longest river reaches the sea, the source of its oil wealth and
scene of unrest. The week before my trip, a group of several hundred
rebels had cut off a third of Nigeria's oil production to press their demands for a fairer share of the oil revenue. Going to the delta, I wanted
to see them and meet their leader.

The cause of the conflict was oil. In 1956, the oil firm Royal
Dutch/Shell struck oil, and, since then, six oil majors and two dozen
smaller firms had set up drilling operations. The region now produces
around 2 million barrels a day, around half of which goes to the United
States. Through this production, Nigeria accounts for 10 percent of
America's oil imports and gets 95 percent of its own foreign earnings.
But while the pipelines that supply this wealth pollute their waters and
land, the people of the delta are poor; they are less likely to go to
school, see a doctor, or find a job than those almost anywhere else in
Nigeria. The people cannot farm or fish, I was told. The waters are
slicked with oil, and the air is choked with fumes. Take a boat out into
the mangrove swamps, and the narrow creeks and muddy banks carry
a sense of menace. These are the brackish waters where men once
traded in slaves.

I arranged my meeting with the rebels through a local politician,
Broderick Bozimo, a leader of the Ijaw people. The next day I went to
the dockside before dawn to wait. Early morning mist still lay on the
water when the young men arrived, the outline of their boat shrouded
in the predawn half-light. After tying up the boat, the youths jumped out
and busied themselves collecting what they needed for the return trip to

the swamps—heaving jerry cans of fuel, water, and other supplies into the boat. They had been there for just five minutes when the man in charge said, "Time to go." These were government waters. He was nervous near land.

Leading the others, he climbed back into the boat, grabbed the starter of the Yamaha outboard motor, and sat down. A cigarette dangled precariously from his fingers over the fuel lines. In his lap, he cradled a pump-action shotgun. I paused, then followed him aboard. The others jumped in. The man pulled the starter, and the boat dipped at the back. Off we went, passing the rusting hulks of abandoned oil tankers, swinging fast and low out of the harbor. Crouched down at the back, I turned around and raised my head to look at the disappearing shoreline. "Keep down," barked the lookout at the front of the boat. "If the navy sees us, they shoot."

"Out there . . ." He pointed to a line somewhere on the horizon up ahead. "Out there we control the waters."

Half an hour later, we pulled into one of the flow stations the rebels had seized, a mass of gleaming metal in a mangrove swamp, used by the oil group Chevron to pump oil to ships offshore. From yards away I could see the reason for the young men's anger. Over the past 40 years, oil firms such as Chevron had made billions in Nigeria. But people like them had gotten nothing. Next to the platform, I saw a run of unadorned huts in the sand: the village some of the men had grown up in. It had no electricity, no school or clinic, no running water, and no bridge to connect it to anywhere. Yet this place made Nigerian soldiers and politicians wealthy and made a fortune for traders like Mai Deribe in the north.

As we approached the shore, I trailed my hand over the side, and my fingers came out covered with a thin oily residue. Fishing, once the cornerstone of the local economy, had become almost impossible, as the fish could not survive in these waters. And the little land available to the villagers was too polluted to grow crops. It was as I'd been told.

I climbed onto the platform and asked a youth what they planned. Bare-chested, perspiration dripping onto the semi-automatic he held in his arms, he knew what he wanted. "Things must change," he said. "The government, the soldiers, must make them change. We are dying here. We have nothing to lose."

Yes, I said. I understood. But what is the plan? What do you want the government to do? Or what will you do?

He misunderstood my question. "If anyone tries to remove us from here, we will blow ourselves up and them too," he said. The others standing around him nodded in agreement, jabbing me to make me look at the rundown homes opposite us, the pollution in the water, the pollution in the sky. "This is why we are here," one said.

I understood the anger but could not see a plan for change. Where was the man in charge? I walked over to the village. There, a soft-spoken 50-year-old fisherman said he could remember the day he first saw men prospecting for oil. "They told us it would cause no problems and would make us rich. We would get roads, bridges, schools, hospitals, jobs. We believed them. But look at this place now," he said. "Farming and fishing are what we have to live on. We can't eat oil."

I was taken to another site, and another, all oil platforms and flow stations owned by companies such as Chevron, Shell, and Exxon Mobil, polluting the waters. Everywhere, the feeling was the same. But I still saw no evidence of change. The rebel leader I'd been planning to meet was more than elusive. He just never showed.

On our return to shore, we were greeted with news of an explosion at a gas pipeline nearby that had killed hundreds. Where was the rebel leader? I asked. I went to see Broderick Bozimo, but he would not say where the leader was. I found out the next day. He was meeting with people from the oil firms, doing a deal that, it turned out, made him rich but did nothing for the people he claimed to lead. It was a betrayal. Days later, the occupations ended and the oil flowed again. For the people of the delta, nothing had changed.

∾

By the end, I'd spent four years in Nigeria. In that time, I'd witnessed hundreds of deaths in towns and cities. I'd seen stupendous wealth amidst numbing poverty. I'd visited rebels fighting—but not changing—the troubled Niger Delta. I'd watched the surging hopes for progress wrecked by politicians in the north and the south.

Around the country, I'd seen much more. I'd seen people laughing, enjoying life, making the most of what they had. But it was not enough. For most people, life was harsh. People were angry, and they were the first to admit it. As Achebe had said, the reason for the troubles they all faced—the constant power cuts, the crime, the corruption, and the poverty—was a failure of leadership.

Unlike many places in the developing world, Nigeria has money and considerable resources. Since independence in 1960, the country has earned billions of dollars from oil and gas. It has, or had, a manufacturing base. It used to be a big agricultural producer. Nigeria's people are hardworking and entrepreneurial. Children pound alongside cars—even in Lagos's notorious downpours—selling trinkets. Men labor on building sites in the heat of a northern day.

But if terrible leadership was the reason for Nigeria's troubles, what was behind it? That was what I needed to know. Nigeria is a place with great potential. But why was it not improving? Was Nigeria condemned to more decades without change?

I set out to explore the reasons. They lie, I believe, in the country's history and culture. They go back to the days of the slave trade, colonial rule, and the move to independence. And I knew then that to understand them required a journey into my family's past.

CHAPTER 3

Conquest

*E*dward Spenser Burns, my great-grandmother's cousin, was born in Paddington, west London, on May 23, 1861. He was the third son and fourth child of a Baptist minister and his wife, Dawson and Cecil Burns. Though the family table, at their home in Tooting, southwest London, was rarely bare, it was not a wealthy household. Edward's grandmother Clara Balfour was the probably illegitimate daughter of a butcher and a seamstress. His grandfather James was a former sailor and recovering alcoholic. But what they lacked in status, the family made up for with drive and ambition.

Well spoken and articulate, Clara, the family matriarch, had set out from a young age to make her mark on society, becoming a prominent public lecturer, a leader of the temperance movement, and an early advocate of women's rights. Edward's mother, Cecil, was the eldest of Clara's children to survive to adulthood. Of her three brothers, John and James went into business, and Jabez, the star and later shame of the family, went into politics as a member of parliament (MP) for two voter districts in central and northern England.

In 1875, when he was 14, Edward graduated from school and was sent across the North Sea to Germany to open his eyes to Europe. He returned a few years later, fluent in German and French, with a taste for travel and a keen interest in the wider world. At first he wanted to enter government service. But when he failed the test, he set off to the other side of the globe, New Zealand, in search of a future. It was his first experience of a society markedly different from his own and a profound culture shock. "In New Zealand," he sniffed in an early letter home, "there is practically no such social distinction as there is in England. And this, I must confess, I do not like for it makes the lower classes—servants, workmen, etcetera—have such a great idea of themselves."[1]

Steady work in New Zealand was hard to come by, and after two years he moved to Australia, where his situation worsened. Suffering dysentery, and with exactly nine pence in his pocket, he staggered 20 miles on foot from Sydney until he reached a farm willing to take him on. His task was "yarding cattle and sheep for the sales for which work my only remuneration is my 'tucker,'" Australian slang for food, he wrote. The experience left him at a rare low ebb. But he soon bounced back and, with the help of a family friend, found enough work to pay his way back to England.

In the summer of 1882, he was off again, this time to America to take up a job with Crook's Mining & Smelting Co., near Lake City, Colorado, a city and a people he liked immediately. But he made enemies at the firm by reporting dishonest accounting practices and lost his position. Then, packed off back to England, he saw an advertisement from a committee working for the Belgian king, Leopold II, offering three-year contracts for work in Africa.

Though Africa was not an obvious choice of destination for a man frequently in poor health, the lure of profit was great for a recently failed cattlehand. And while the West today looks on Africa as a place of war, disease, and suffering, end-of-the-century Europe saw it as a place of opportunity. Africa then was the fabled home of the Ashanti goldmines and the diamond fields of South Africa.

∽

The Africa Burns found was one shaped by its history. It was a continent of kingdoms, caliphates, and city-states that long predated his arrival, a continent that would have developed very differently but for the intervention of the Europeans four centuries earlier.

When Burns arrived in Africa, the territory that is today Nigeria had been home to people for almost 40,000 years. Arriving there from the north, they had wandered the plains for millennia and settled down. Over the course of the past 3,000 years, they had formed the first modern states. Of those, one in particular stood out for its wealth and staying power: the northern Kanem-Borno Empire, established around 850 A.D. on the southern fringes of Lake Chad and still flourishing more than a thousand years later.

In the eleventh century, it introduced Islam to the region and became a noted center of Islamic learning. By the twelfth century, it was strong enough to send caravans across the desert to the rulers of Cairo, Tunis, and Marrakech. Kanem-Borno's position on the trans-Saharan trade routes assured it control of trade in gold, ivory, salt, and slaves, and it prospered as a result. In the mid–sixteenth century, its ruler created a new administration, set up better schools, and strengthened the army, creating a cavalry drawn from the nobility and armed and trained by Turkish musketeers. He combined this with an infantry, a peasant rabble armed with bows, arrows, and spears, and used it to expand the borders of the empire. Powerful, autocratic, and effective, Kanem-Borno marked the first flourishing of a northern political tradition.

Soon after Kanem-Borno was formed, other states emerged in the north and south. In the north, seven major cities were founded by the

Hausas between 1000 and 1200 A.D. Their rulers—the Hausa kings, or *sarki*—formed standing armies, levied taxes on farmers and traders to pay for them and their administrations, and built stout city walls to guard against attacks by their rivals. Over the centuries, their rulers adopted Islam, in name at least. They also developed the practice of autocratic rule.

Meanwhile, in the south, the Yoruba people were forming kingdoms in the forests of the southwest. The most powerful was Oyo. Its ruler, the *alafin,* raised an army that defeated all opponents and established Oyo's dominance over the other Yoruba states. But, unlike the rulers of Kanem-Borno and the Hausa cities, the alafin's power was not absolute, but tempered by the interventions of a seven-strong people's council. And there and elsewhere in the south, the people generally had a greater say in government than those in the north.

As the centuries passed, these societies developed politically, socially, and culturally. And had they continued to develop unhindered, it is clear that something very different from what we see today would have formed in what is now Nigeria. Instead of the country created by the British, six or seven states would have emerged. The Yoruba would perhaps have welcomed the arrival of the missionaries and their Western education, but on their own terms. A Hausa caliphate would have continued in the north. A city-state would have emerged from the powerful Benin kingdom in the south. There would have been a separate country for the Igbo people of the southeast and a federation of states for the coastal peoples of the Niger Delta. Kanem-Borno would have survived in the far northwest. There was a process of state-building and border formation taking place, and that would have gone on.[2]

It was not to be, and for one reason above all: the coming of the trans-Atlantic slave trade.

❦

The Atlantic trade in slaves, launched by the Portuguese in the fifteenth century and pursued vigorously by them, the Dutch, the French, and the British for almost 400 years, forced more than 10 million men, women, and children out of Africa, scattering families and transforming the fates of countless individuals and peoples worldwide. If Africa as a whole was the part of the world most affected by the slave trade, few parts of Africa felt its effects more deeply than the area that is Nigeria today.

For the slave trade, the area that is now Nigeria had two big draws. First was geography. The region lies in easy reach across the Atlantic from Europe and the Americas and has a series of deep-water ports such as Lagos that make for easy landings for ships. Second was population. What is today Nigeria was already, by the fifteenth century, a heavily populated area, rich in prospective slaves and people willing to sell them. So, lying where it did and being home to a large population, Nigeria was central to the slave trade; home to one-third of all those shipped as slaves to the Americas.[3]

The first to suffer from this calamity were, of course, the millions wrenched from their families, taken in chains and shackles, and beaten aboard ships to live or die in new lands. Of these horrors, there are many painful accounts. One of the most striking, though its details are disputed by some,[4] is that of a young Nigerian, Olaudah Equiano, seized as a slave in 1756, at the age of 11. According to his account, Equiano was separated from his sister, marched to the sea, taken aboard a ship, weighed, and poked. "The first object that saluted my eyes when I arrived on the coast was the sea and a slave ship . . . a multitude of black people of every description chained together, every one of their countenances expressing dejection and sorrow," he later wrote.[5]

The young Equiano said he survived the rigors of the trans-Atlantic journey and was sold in Virginia to a British naval officer. He became the officer's personal attendant and traveled frequently, often participating in major naval battles. He learned English and became an accomplished sailor in his own right. He also became a Christian and was allowed to trade on his own account when in port. Eventually, this earned him enough to buy his freedom and sail for England, where he joined the growing campaign against the slave trade.

At the time, eradicating slavery was still a political pipe dream. Popular opinion followed the rationale of the slave traders: that slavery had always existed around the world and that Africa offered no exception. Since slavery was practiced in Africa, the enslavement of Africans overseas was no crime, the traders claimed. Of course, what they failed to add was that, in most parts of Africa, the nature of slavery was very different from that seen elsewhere. In Africa, "The slave in most interior districts is treated with infinitely greater leniency and kindness than the slaves of European planters" in the Caribbean, the British explorer Richard Lander wrote after traveling in Nigeria in 1830. "Upon the whole, I should consider the situation of domestic slaves in Africa to be more enviable than that of the household servant in Europe," he added.[6] And on this he spoke with rare authority—he too had been a domestic servant in Britain.

However, if the position of slaves in the interior was better than that of slaves elsewhere, the nearer that they got to the sea, the worse it became. This was the "debasing effect" of the trade, which critics such as Lander denounced.[7] For the closer to the coast it was, the more involved a community was likely to be in the trade in slaves, and the more involved it was in the slave trade, the more brutal society was in general. And nowhere was this effect felt more strongly than in places such as the ports of Lagos and Bonny in the Niger Delta, the areas most involved in the trade. In Badagry, a small port near the western borders of what is today Nigeria, Lander reported seeing captured slave runaways dangling from trees. The treatment of those who did not flee was just as brutal, he wrote: they were chained up, whipped, and left for dead if their owner believed they had transgressed.

Had the slave trade brutalized the Niger Delta? I asked Chief Harold Dappe-Biriye, a prominent delta leader in 1998, a man whose Itsekiri people were once deeply involved in the trade. "Of course it did," he said, sitting blinking in his home in Port Harcourt, curtains drawn to keep out the harsh light of day. "Our people got the guns. We went out and got the people we needed: boys and girls. They came to work for us, or to be sold. It was not nice. But it was the morality of the time. If you were stronger than someone, you mastered him. That was all." And since then? "It still has its effects. The Delta is a harsh place, the harshest in Nigeria. If someone is weak, you master them. It is as before."

The slave trade changed society in Nigeria.

∾

The effect of the trade was felt not only on human relations. In Europe and the Americas, the trade brought prosperity to owners and shippers. In Europe, the profits on a slaving trip would rise in the mid-nineteenth century, when the trade was banned but continued regardless, to £10,000,[8] equivalent to more than £7 million today.[9] In Africa, too, the trade made some men rich and empowered them as rulers, upsetting the balance of power in states across Nigeria and turning many of them into despots.

In the north, the rule of the Hausa kings became unpopular through the seventeenth and eighteenth centuries because of the constant slave-raiding and high taxes they imposed on the people. In 1804, an Islamic scholar named Usman dan Fodio emerged in one northern state and declared a Holy War to overthrow all the Hausa kings and set up an Islamic caliphate to rule in their place. When he began his campaign, the kings found little support among the Hausa peasantry. The people had not themselves risen against their rulers, but they wanted an end to the slave-raiding and despotic rule they had suffered.[10] Between 1804 and 1808, the Hausa states all fell one by one to new rulers. And under Fodio, an Islamic caliphate was formed that would run the north for the rest of the century.

At the same time, the increasing despotism of the Oyo Empire was sowing division among the Yoruba states in the southwest and within the Benin Kingdom further east. Slave-raiding was common. And, around 1820, wars broke out between the Yorubas that would end only 70 years later, when the British imposed their rule over them. The destabilizing effect of the slave trade had, it seemed, played a big part in the collapse of the system of Yoruba rule.

As this was happening, the effort to end the slave trade, launched in England at the tail end of the eighteenth century, was coming to a head. In February 1807, when the last Hausa city-states were falling to Fodio's forces, a bill to abolish the slave trade was presented to the House of Commons in London. Backed by a coalition of politicians, judges, and bishops, it finally triumphed, passing by 283 votes to 16, bringing to a climax a 30-year campaign to end the trade.

To end the trade, which was still being carried on by other nations, the British set up a base and announced a blockade of the African coast. Ships carrying slaves would be stopped and their cargo returned to shore. The ships themselves would be confiscated, the owners were told. The measures sounded tough, but after three decades, it was clear the blockade was not working. In the slave markets of the Americas, the price of slaves had risen because of prohibition. This meant owners were willing to risk confiscation of their ships and cargo for the profits they could make when the ships did get through. So campaigners proposed a new tactic—to shut down the trade at the source, seizing control of land on the African coast to do so.

In Nigeria, the first target of the new policy, agreed on by London, was Lagos, the biggest of the ports on the West African coast. "The slave trade on that part of the African coast would be at an end if Lagos, the stronghold of its greatest support, was destroyed," Samuel Ajayi Crowther told Britain's Queen Victoria in 1850.[11] Crowther, a former Yoruba slave who converted to Christianity and returned to Nigeria in 1841 as an emissary of the Church Missionary Society, was an active proponent of colonization. He was far from alone. Others who campaigned for the British to take Lagos were traders, eager to expand the opportunities for trade, and officials, fearful of encroachment by the French. And finally, in November 1851, the government bowed to the pressure and ordered its consul, John Beecroft, the head of the fleet enforcing the British ban on the slave trade, to sail for Lagos. There, he was told, he was to persuade the *oba,* or king, to sign a treaty stopping the selling of slaves in Lagos and to open the port to British trade. Failing that, he was to take control of the city.

On arrival at Lagos, the consul was immediately snubbed by the oba. Rightly fearful of British intentions, the Yoruba king ordered his guns to turn on the British ships. Affronted, Beecroft asked London for orders and was given permission to attack. Two days after Christmas, on December 27, 1851, he did so. A shell then set off a fire that destroyed much of the town.[12] The old oba fled, and a new, pro-British oba was installed.

Britain was starting to take hold but its control was still tenuous. A decade later, London went further, announcing the formal annexation of the city. The reasons it gave were that the slave trade still continued and the need to avert the risk of France extending its control. Threatened with removal from office if he resisted, the new oba of Lagos ceded control of the city to London. And at a ceremony in the British consulate, the Union Jack was unfurled, troops came ashore, and 300 local children sang a rather tuneless version of "God Save the Queen." It was 1862. Lagos was a British colony at last.

Over the next few years, doubts began to emerge in London about the wisdom of taking more land in the region. With the colonization of Lagos, slave rebellions in the Americas, and the defeat of the South in America's Civil War, the trafficking of slaves finally stopped. And with problems elsewhere in the world to deal with, a select committee of the House of Commons in 1865 urged an end to the colonization of West Africa and a withdrawal from existing colonies. Enough had now been done to end the slave trade, the MPs said.

That did not happen, but, in 1882, the colonial secretary Lord Kimberley, a Liberal, set out further arguments against extending British rule into the interior. "The coast is pestilential; the natives numerous and unmanageable. The result of a British occupation would be almost certainly wars with the natives and heavy demands upon the British taxpayer," he wrote to William Gladstone, then prime minister.[13]

British opinion was divided. While the Liberal Kimberley opposed further colonization of the region, his Tory counterpart Joseph Chamberlain was actively promoting it and, in 1885, the Conservatives returned to office. Chamberlain's concern was that, if Britain did not act to claim more land along the coast, London's great rival, Paris, would take control of the greater part of the continent. And a decade after Kimberley left office, Britain would come close to war with France to defend its claims, as all across Africa, spurred by a coalition of traders, missionaries, and officials, Britain raced to join the European land-grab on the continent.

∽

Edward Burns's employer from 1883, the International African Association, or IAA, was an unscrupulous organization. It had been formed in

September 1876 when King Leopold II, the new Belgian monarch, invited to Brussels a distinguished group of explorers, humanitarians, and philanthropists. The goal, he claimed, was the creation of an organization capable of eradicating slavery and furthering the advance of European science and learning in a large part of Central Africa. Its purpose, he said, would be to "open to civilization the only part of our globe which it has not yet penetrated, to pierce the darkness which hangs over entire peoples."[14]

However, Leopold's real aims were anything but noble or selfless. He ordered the IAA to claim control of land across the Congo, and then he used a string of companies he secretly controlled to exploit the region's people and its ivory, rubber, and other resources. Personal kingly wealth was his only concern, not the emancipation or the advancement of the African people.

In his goals, he was not unusual. At the time the king set up his association, the other European powers were doing the same thing, from the British on the Niger to the French on the Ivory Coast and in Senegal and the Portuguese in Angola and Mozambique. The Belgian king simply did not want to miss out. "I do not want to miss a good chance of getting us a slice of this magnificent African cake," he told an aide in 1877.[15]

But to secure his claim, the IAA needed men eager to make both a living and a name for themselves, in Africa or elsewhere. It needed foot soldiers. And in November 1883, that is what Edward Burns became.

∾

If Burns was worried by the challenges he faced, he failed to show it. The portrait I have of him at that time, sketched by a family member a few days before he sailed, shows a determined young man, his hair neatly parted, his mouth unsmiling, partly hidden under a handlebar mustache, his gaze disappearing off into the distance, nervous perhaps, but firm about his decision.

Going to Africa, Burns knew he risked his health. Since the earliest visits by Portuguese traders and explorers, West Africa had gained a reputation as a graveyard for Europeans. With quinine identified as a weapon to fight malaria, the health risks associated with the region had diminished. But malaria was not the area's only endemic disease. Taken together, malaria, dysentery, cholera, and a host of other diseases were responsible for killing a third of those who worked for the association in the Congo at that time.[16]

Determined not to be put off, Edward dismissed his family's concerns about his health. And on November 13, 1883, he took a train for Liverpool and boarded the boat for Africa. "I am feeling very well and am taking care of myself," he wrote the next week as the ship traveled south. "I have a cold salt water bath each morning, a plentiful supply of quinine, and do not expose myself in the burning sun more than necessary," he told his brother Len in a letter home.

But the danger to his health was not the only risk that Edward ran. The other was that of failure. After earlier setbacks in New Zealand, Australia, and America, he needed to establish his career in Africa. Even before he left for the Congo, Edward had indicated to his uncle Jabez an interest in an eventual appointment working for the British on the Niger River. That was his goal, once he had proven himself to the Belgians in the Congo.

∾

The trip to Africa was Edward's first to the continent, and it was clear immediately that he had much to learn there. The worldview at home in Tooting, London, was neither open nor broadminded in those days. A young man full of racial and national pride, Edward wrote home from the ship referring to those he saw ashore as people of "inferior races." In language that was then common, he told his mother that the ship had been calling at places "for the purpose of picking up niggers who work on board." It was "quite a joke to watch them," he said, mocking the dress and mannerisms of those he saw.

After a stop in Sierra Leone and his brief venture into Nigeria, he arrived on Christmas Eve at Loango, the capital of a Congolese kingdom founded in the fifteenth century that stretched from Mayombe in the north to near the mouth of the Congo River in the south. But Edward knew and cared little about the kingdom's history. He was not there to learn about Africa, nor to assist it, but to claim it for the king. And, after spending Christmas and the New Year with his colleagues, he set to work, leading out a company of soldiers and porters, all traveling under the association's blue flag with a yellow star, to wipe the kingdom of Loango from the map.

The party that Edward led out on January 2, 1884, was 70 strong in total. The 22-year-old Edward and a colleague, Captain Ellison, were in joint command of 30 African soldiers and 40 local porters. The troops assembled at five o'clock in the morning to leave before dawn and beat the heat. Their orders were to take possession of the country as far north of Loango as they could get and to halt a move south by the French.

For the first four days, the going was tough. Sweat ran in rivers down their arms as they hacked their way 75 miles north before they decided that it was too difficult for the party as a whole, and Edward set out ahead with a smaller group while his colleague secured the rear. Edward was making for a place called Banda Point, a key location the association was desperate to claim to ensure its access to a major part of the interior. His task there was to convince its rulers to cede sovereignty to the IAA by signing a paper "treaty," written in foreign legalese, declaring that they were giving up their title to the land and ceding it to the Belgian crown.

"We arrived at three in the afternoon after a journey due East through a beautiful country of alternating bush and grassland," Edward wrote in a letter to his mother. It was his first view of the African interior, and he was struck by its richness. "Everywhere something grows, a bird calls, an animal can be heard," he wrote.

From Banda Point, he had a further day's journey to the village where he would meet the local king and negotiate the signing of the treaty. He arrived just after midday. "The king, the poor old boy, seemed on his last legs," Edward wrote that night. Elderly though he was, the man was neither a fool, nor naïve. The king said he was worried that Edward was French, whom he had heard were seizing land across the region. Edward assured him he was not French but British, and an enemy of the French. He was there as a friend to offer gifts of cloth and money and the protection of the association. All that was needed was a signature, or mark, on a piece of paper. Then the gifts he'd brought and the protection of the association would be his.

The king thought about it for a while, consulted, and "readily affixed his mark." He was, Edward wrote, "delighted with the old cloak he got in return." Pleased with himself, Edward set off back to Banda Point within the hour. As the king saw him go, he could not have known that, to the rulers in Europe, he had just signed away control of his land.

A hundred miles further north, at Sette Camma, the task was not quite as easy. The day after returning to Banda Point, a small coastal steamer arrived and took the party aboard, carrying them up to Mayumba, further along on the coast. As the steamer was going on, it was decided that Edward would travel with it to Sette Camma, an important rubber-trading post that had not yet been claimed by any of the European powers. The trip took two more days. The party arrived and took possession of the trading house. "Our flag, blue with a yellow star, is flying at the flagstaff, as a sign that the Association is in possession," Edward wrote.

However, the rulers at Sette Camma were wise to Edward's designs, having dealt with Europeans for many years, and were reluctant to sign the treaty he had brought in his bags without some guarantees.

First, they said, they too were worried that Burns might be French and planning on seizing their land. "You say you are an Englishman, and we heard you talk like an Englishman. But you don't carry the English flag. In fact, we never saw a flag like yours before," the elderly town chief told him, suspiciously, when he obtained a meeting. The treaty that he had proffered was written in French. "And still you say you are not French and are come here to prevent the French people from having our country. We want to know who you really are."

Edward explained his position but could not persuade the old man into signing. He was rebuffed. The offer of gifts was rejected too. So when discussions and trinkets would not work, Burns resorted to the threat of force.

"As we talked, I ordered out from the bush my full company of soldiers, all heavily armed and with bayonets drawn, to stand behind me. 'These men show the protection I could offer,' I said, but only if the old chief signed. If he refused, 'there would be a battle,'" Edward wrote. And he did not need to spell out the argument any further. The chief understood.

"Soon, we got the treaty signed, hoisted our flag over the town, fired seven salutes from a cannon, and gave ourselves a hearty feed. I must say, I like this sort of thing immensely," Edward wrote that night.

❧

In this one area alone, the association operated five stations like Edward's, each with its own officers and men. Across the Congo, hundreds of

Europeans and thousands of locals were employed. Abuse of company employees, and the civilian population, was commonplace. The lowest-ranked staff, such as porters, suffered the worst.

After returning to Loango with two treaties signed, Edward's next assignment, in mid-February, was to be sent to the interior to open the route to a major new trading post. Shortly before noon the next day, he assembled his men—30 soldiers and 40 porters—and set out. Climbing a range of hills at the back of the station, he took an easterly course over hilly country and reached the village of Tcheles m'Fur at about five o'clock in the evening, and camped for the night, he reported in the expedition's log. The next day, the journey took him across undulating plains to the mountain border of the Kwilu Valley. From there, the path climbed for six days and took the party into Mayombe County. And this was where the problems began.

As they walked, word came down the line that hostile locals lay ahead. When Edward gave the order to march, the porters refused to stir and demanded to be allowed to return home. He refused. If the porters returned, he would have had to return too, and the trip would have failed. He'd have lost both time and his reputation with his employers. So he gathered the soldiers behind him and, when reasoning and joking with the porters failed, he threatened them with a flogging.

The threats failed. As Edward turned to grab his cane, 25 of the porters deserted, turning in a moment and disappearing into the bush. Edward heard them go, grabbed his gun instead, and shot over their heads. When that failed to stop their flight, he sent out a party of soldiers after them. By noon the next day, 20 had been brought back, and by nightfall, the last man was brought in. For the ringleaders, Edward ordered 35 lashes each, and for the other men 25. All would receive half-rations for the rest of the trip. And for the future, "I made them distinctly understand that I would order the soldiers to fire on any man trying to desert."

Such treatment of hired men was common all across Africa. Arriving seven weeks later at Manyanga, on the Congo River, Edward walked in to the station to meet the famed explorer H. M. Stanley, head of the IAA mission in the Congo. Stanley, originally from Wales but a naturalized American who had fought on both sides in the Civil War, was known around the world for tracking down the explorer Dr. David Livingstone in the bush, ten years earlier. In Britain, he was considered a national hero.

After Edward's arrival, the two first discussed the route the young man had taken, then the tough stance he had taken with the porters. The old Africa hand backed his approach. It was not for nothing that Stanley was known in the Congo as Bulu Matari, or "the stone-breaker," a star-struck Edward later claimed. Stanley, he added, had asked him to write a report for King Leopold on his trip. The next month, Edward would be named a member of the Royal Geographical Society for the reports of his exploration.

∽

At first, Edward had no doubts about what the association was doing in the Congo. Flattered just to be asked to write a report to the king of Belgium, the young man had accepted from the outset Leopold's description of the operation of which he was now part. "His object is the philanthropic one of opening up the centre of Africa to European civilization and trade," Edward wrote in a letter to a former schoolteacher that month. "We do not trade ourselves, so the king gets no return for all his outlay," he asserted. The king hoped only to witness the "peaceful development and progress of these simple people," so the company gave every encouragement to honest traders and to missionaries, he said.

Unfortunately, this depiction was patently untrue. As he wrote the words, the association was buying up ivory and would soon start forcing locals into harvesting rubber, a trade practice that would kill many hundreds of thousands of Congolese over the following decades. Within a few years, the association was making the king more money than he could spend, earning him a fortune estimated at the equivalent of more than a billion dollars within a decade.[17] And, over that same period, the population of the Congo shrank by 5–8 million because of disease, starvation, and mass killing by Belgian agents.[18]

Though he was at first proud of his work for the association—leading expeditions and signing up treaties—Edward eventually began to question the way it worked. Initially, he was critical of his European colleagues. The Belgians were "incompetent," the young Englishman charged. Often they appeared in league with the "lazy" Portuguese and "unprincipled" French. The worst qualities of the latter had been shown by the French empire-builder Pierre de Brazza. "We know too well how the agents of Brazza have secured their territories in this part of Africa. If a king shows any disinclination to sign a treaty with them, a pistol is held at his head, and he is given his choice between signing or being shot," Edward complained.

In fact, as his first dealings had shown, the young Englishman was not averse to using threats himself.

A few months after his posting to Manyanga, Edward was ordered south to a small town called N'Lungi, after a villager shot one of his soldiers. Such attacks were a challenge to the association's authority, his superior officer said, and ordered him to investigate.

Reaching the place about midday, he found it deserted. After a while, a nervous man appeared, sent by the chiefs to inform the white man that he should leave. Edward said no, he would stay, planning to wait out the community if he had to, knowing they had to return soon to get water. A few hours later, the chiefs returned with their people and supporters.

"I told them what I had come for," he wrote. "They could choose to be friends or enemies." If they chose to be friends, he would make a treaty and give presents. If they decided to be enemies, he would settle the matter at once and "decide who was the stronger." The chiefs looked at his assembled soldiers with their fast-loading rifles and back at their own men. They agreed to sign.

But soon Edward began to question seriously what he, too, was doing in Africa, and not just how the Belgians and the French were operating. When the residents of one village fled at his approach, he was struck by their fear at the arrival of a European. He persuaded a group to return, and they talked for hours into the night. "For years, the white man's coming has been the signal for crime, for robbery of the worst kind, for slaughter and still worse, years of unrequited toil and captivity and finally a grave in a foreign land," he wrote in a letter to his old schoolteacher the following month. Betraying for a first time a trace of empathy for a people he had so scorned months earlier, he added: "I put myself in the place of the black and wondered what would my feelings be if my home had been burnt, my fields trampled on, my father and brothers murdered before my eyes, my mother and sister driven off with blows of a cruel lash into foreign lands and endless captivity. And agitated by such thoughts I lay tossing and turning through the whole of that long, calm, African night."

∾

His first year in Africa was ending, and Edward was increasingly unhappy working for the association. He was suspicious of the aims of the Belgian crown and, in the last months of the year, he started again to look into the prospects of work in Nigeria, an area under growing British control. In November, he heard that the post of consul on the upper reaches of the River Niger was available and he applied. Delayed by a storm off the Bay of Biscay, his application for the post arrived too late at the Colonial Office in London. But he was told through his uncle, the politician and MP Jabez Balfour, that he had been accepted for the post when it next became available. "Then," he wrote to his parents, "I should be the representative of England on that river, sent there to put down the large slave trade which is now being carried on, for that is the object that the government has for the position." That, of course, was not the main British motive for colonization in 1884, but Edward thought it was. And, with the way he now viewed the association, it gave him further reason to leave.

His work of signing up treaties—12 in all—was almost done. At the end of that year, delegates from across Europe and the United States were called to Berlin by Germany's chancellor, Otto von Bismarck. For many months now, great power agents had been staking claims to trading rights all across Africa, acquiring "treaties" that conferred a paper legitimacy on the British, Belgian, and other claims to places such as Nigeria and the Congo. Bismarck, the Iron Chancellor, wanted to ensure that the process could continue while avoiding a European war over Africa. And the congress in Berlin was to achieve that goal.

If Burns had regrets, it was too late. And at the start of February 1885, Edward fell sick. He wrote to his brother Len that a friend and colleague had suddenly died and it had left him depressed and worried. He feared he had picked up an infection himself. He had been ill for a month with three fevers in quick succession, the latter two of them "decidedly bilious." He decided to return to the coast, but his decision came too late to save him.

The news the family did not want to hear came from W. P. Tisdel, the American representative to the new government of the Congo.

"Dear Sir," read the letter that Tisdel sent via the House of Commons, "I have to announce to you the death of E. Spenser Burns." He had died at Leopoldville, on the banks of the River Congo. The two men had been traveling together. As Edward weakened, he had had to be carried in a hammock slung between the shoulders of the porters. They had tried to get him to the coast, but the fever had taken too deep a hold. "It was impossible to keep him." He died on March 1, 1885. He was 23 years old.

The London papers wrote obituaries. H. M. Stanley, the national hero, wrote the family a letter, calling Edward a "very superior person" and proclaiming his death a great loss to the association. That was of little comfort to the family. His work, for a cause he perhaps misunderstood, in a place he most certainly misunderstood, had cost him his life. It had also unjustly deprived many people of the Congo of their freedom. With the flimsy legitimacy of the treaties he had persuaded their leaders to sign, he had played his part in its colonization. He had helped destroy the old and set the new borders of Africa.

CHAPTER 4

Another Man's Home

In Nigeria, the people driving colonization were much like those for whom Edward Burns worked, and the process they used was much the same. Born in 1846 to a wealthy family on the Isle of Man, a small island off the coast of northern England, Sir George Dashwood Taubman Goldie was not a king like Leopold. But, as his Belgian counterpart had done in the Congo, he founded a commercial empire in Nigeria and set the borders of a country, using men like Edward Burns to do it.

A smart but wayward youth, Sir George had flunked out of school as a child, spent time adventuring with the army in Egypt and Sudan, and run off with the family governess by the time he was in his early twenties. His thirtieth birthday approaching, and despairing of his prospects, his parents tasked him with rescuing a failing family-owned palm oil firm, Holland Jacques, in the Niger Delta. And with that single act, they changed his life forever: Sir George became a palm oil tycoon and, some would say, the man who made Nigeria.

Palm oil, the stock-in-trade of Holland Jacques, was the main so-called legitimate produce of Nigeria the year Goldie went out to Nigeria, legitimate insofar as its trading practices were a notch better than those of the slave trade, but only a notch. Often produced in the sort of slave plantations Burns later visited on his way to the Congo, palm oil was highly sought after in Europe then to make candles, soaps, and lubricants for industry. And, as Goldie saw, the trade in palm oil had all the essentials needed to make it a profitable business for the European firms that bought it in Africa and sold it in Europe, save for one problem: the price they paid for it in the delta, where an effective cartel of delta middlemen had driven up prices.

Going out to the delta in 1875, Goldie realized immediately that with many firms competing for the same stock, the delta middlemen who controlled access to the plantations had the upper hand in the business. This was something he was determined to change—and he did, forging partnerships with the main British firms to force the middlemen to sell at prices he set.

For Goldie, however, the level of profit was still not enough. Like Leopold in the Congo, he decided that to exploit his opportunities to the maximum, he needed full control over trade with the region. So, like Leopold, he hired agents like Burns to pressure local rulers into signing "treaties" ceding sovereignty and trading rights to his company and the Crown. And, at the Berlin Conference in 1885, Goldie's National Africa Company secured the agreement of Europe to oversee trade in the territory soon to become Nigeria, and set its borders.

∞

As Goldie extended his control over what would soon become Nigeria, a handful of local rulers offered important, if ultimately futile, resistance to his growing rule. In 1884, King Jaja of Opobo, a former Igbo slave who had made himself a local king of the palm oil trade, refused to sign any agreement with Goldie or the Crown until he had a letter affirming that his sovereignty would not be threatened. Wielding power in the creeks, he continued to block British trade even when the letter was written, until, fooled into meeting a British negotiating party, he was seized by Crown troops, put on a ship, and forcibly exiled to the West Indies.

In 1885, a more serious challenge occurred. Goldie's company had brought the delta town of Brass to the brink of starvation by preventing its people from trading. The town's people had pleaded with the company to ease its monopoly on trade but without success. So, in January that year, the town's ruler, King Koko, led a war party in an attack on the company's delta headquarters at Akassa, at the southern tip of the delta. Emerging from the mist in a fleet of dugout canoes, the assailants killed more than 40 company employees, seized dozens more as prisoners, and took them back to Brass, where a number were ritually slaughtered and eaten.

The revolt in Brass, though far from unique, was particularly significant because of its scale and the attention it drew to conditions for locals under Goldie's rule. For while British officials condemned the attack and ordered punishment for the town, the outcry made those in London realize that something was terribly wrong with the way Goldie's company was operating. From Whitehall's perspective, the manner of its operations was putting the company at risk of becoming a national embarrassment.

At the same time, officials in London were becoming nervous at the prospect of France increasing its influence in Nigeria if the country remained under Goldie's control. And traders in Lagos and elsewhere were agitating for London to extend its rule into Yorubaland and beyond, where continuing warfare between the Yoruba kingdoms was hindering the development of trade with the new British colony of Lagos.

Together, this pressure from traders, national rivalry with France, and political concerns at home were pushing London to extend its control. In 1892, Sir Gilbert Carter, the British governor of Lagos, ordered a military expedition to overcome the main Yoruba kingdom that was still blocking the advance of British trade and then set off the next year on a tour of Yoruba states to negotiate free passage for British trade and an end to all inter-Yoruba fighting. To Samuel Johnson, a historian, freed former slave, and eager ally of the British, this extension of British rule, bringing an end to years of Yoruba conflict, brought great relief to the population. "To the vast majority of the common people, it was like the opening of a prison door. No one who witnessed it . . . could refrain from heaving a sigh of gratification," he wrote.[1] Yoruba leaders would later rue their easy acceptance of British rule. Failing to come together, they had fallen to outsiders. But, by the time they realized this, it was much too late. The British had taken over.

Piece by piece, southern Nigeria was coming under the Crown. Benin, the ancient kingdom lying east of Lagos, at the fringes of the Niger Delta, was captured in 1897 after a brief battle, despite a failed attempt by the oba to ward off the British attack with a wave of sacrifices. Tired of his increasingly bloody reign, many of his subjects too welcomed British rule.

Now the rest would follow. Finally, on the first day of 1900, London moved to formalize its control over the territory claimed earlier for Britain by the trader Goldie. As the new century dawned, the government rescinded Goldie's charter, paying him and his company £450,000[2] in compensation, more than £200 million in today's money. And with that, it took over administration of the twin regions of north and south Nigeria, the newest parts of the British Empire. The way he ran the company had caused outrage to some. But to most of his countrymen Goldie was a national hero for the way he had succeeded in acquiring for Britain control of such a large stretch of territory on either side of the River Niger. Securing hundreds of treaties ceding power to the company and the Crown, he had kept out the French and set the shape of Nigeria. Now London needed to find governors for the north and south.

ॐ

In the south, London named as governor Sir Ralph Moor, a Colonial Office veteran with a solid reputation. British policy at the time was that all its colonies should be self-funding, the people of the territories covering the cost of their own colonization through taxes, labor, and duties on trade. Nigeria, north and south, was to be no exception. As the British well knew, the region had long had its own systems of trade and currency. To make it pay for its upkeep, the colonial system introduced taxes, waged and forced labor, and trade in cash crops. If southern Nigeria was to develop, the Treasury wanted it run at no cost to the British.

In the north, the challenge was different. Parts of the south had been under British rule for almost 40 years. But, when the government took over in 1900, only three northern districts—Ilorin, Borgu, and Kabba—were under effective British control, and the leaders of the seven major cities, including Sokoto and Kano, were openly hostile to further British advance. Trade, the lifeblood of the empire that paid for its administration, was negligible. It would have to be fostered. But first, most of the north would have to be conquered.

Born in 1858 in Madras, India, Sir Frederick Lugard, the governor appointed for the north—and the other Briton with a claim to be founder of Nigeria—was a soldier experienced in fighting colonial wars. The son of a British army chaplain and his wife, a minor British aristocrat, Lugard had grown up set on following his father into either the army or the cloth. The decision was made when, still a teenager, he won entry to the most prestigious British army college, Sandhurst, in

Berkshire, southern England. From there, he was commissioned into the East Norfolk Regiment at the age of 20. And taking quickly to army life, he served with distinction in campaigns in Afghanistan, Sudan, and Burma and looked determined to continue an army career.

However, in 1887, when he was 29, he was betrayed in love and suffered a breakdown that almost brought his career to an end. The cause was his relationship with a woman, a divorcée known to friends as Clytie, the first serious love of his life. Lugard was in Burma when he heard reports that his lover was at death's door after an accident in Lucknow, India. Fearing the worst, he rushed to her home, only to find her well enough to have left for London. Following her there, he discovered her, much recovered, in bed with another man.[3] Distraught at this betrayal, Lugard was inconsolable, resigned his commission, and set off on a trip he determined would be his last: a trip halfway around the world to Africa. It was a trip that was to shape his life and Nigeria.

Lugard's journey took him first to Uganda, where, looking for suitable work, he joined the services of the British East Africa Company, an imperial trading company along the lines of the ones run in India and elsewhere in Africa in those days. But once there, rather than fight and die as he had hoped, Lugard fought with distinction and success, making his name helping to establish the British company's rule in East Africa and fight off the French. Indeed, such was his success in Uganda that, when the campaign was over, both Goldie and London would seek him out as the man to lead expeditions to northern Nigeria.

Claiming territory for Britain in Africa was work that Lugard believed in for many reasons. According to Lugard's friend and biographer, Margery Perham, Goldie and Lugard were men of like minds when it came to colonial rule. "The first duty they knew was to their own country, to make her strong and prosperous and to uphold her power and honor," she said.[4] But more than that, Lugard believed that bringing

Africa under British rule was the moral thing to do. Colonization, he believed, brought the continent the "Three Cs"—commerce, Christianity, and civilization—espoused a decade earlier by David Livingstone. In Africa, Lugard saw a place of great poverty, ignorance, and cruelty, and believed that the greatest good would be for it to come under European rule. The "short, sharp" military actions this required were a minor price for Africans to pay.

Now governor of the north, the task facing Lugard in 1900 was easier than it seemed for a number of reasons. One was weaponry. Three years earlier, London had set up a small unit under Lugard's command—the West Africa Frontier Force—composed of around 200 European officers and 2,000 African men to impose control on the region. The force was certainly small in number for so large an area. But, as the British satirist Hilaire Belloc noted, it had a weapon, an early version of the machine gun known as the Maxim gun, that gave all who wielded it a clear battlefield advantage.

> *Whatever happens we have got,*
> *The Maxim Gun, and they have not,*

the aptly named antihero William Blood declares in Belloc's mock-colonial poem *The Modern Traveller.*[5]

But advantage though it was, the Maxim gun was not decisive. Lugard's campaign to take the north started in 1900. First, a company of troops was sent up from his headquarters at Lokoja, a town at the junction of Nigeria's two great rivers, to topple the emirs of Nupe and Kontagora, emirates that had refused to stop slave trading and were thought to have limited support from the population. So it proved. Resistance was limited. Soon other emirates followed, all toppled easily, putting up little fight. And by the middle of the next year, eight northern and central provinces were under Lugard's control. And by 1902, Abuja, the current capital, and Keffi had also fallen to the troops Lugard sent out against them.

However, to impose himself on northern Nigeria, Lugard still needed to control Kano and Sokoto, the two most powerful cities in the north. Kano was the larger of the two, busier and noisier, home to more than 40,000 people. In 1824, when the British explorer Captain Hugh Clapperton had visited, most of its people still lived within its ancient city walls, in large walled compounds built, he said, in a Moorish style. The population was broadly divided between farmers, going out to tend crops in the fields, and traders, selling everything from gold and incense to cattle and slaves. The slave market was held in two long sheds, one for men, the other for women. The slaves, he said, were "seated in rows and carefully decked out for exhibition. Young or old, plump or withered, beautiful or ugly are sold without distinction."[6] Kano was the first major target.

Sokoto, further north and west, on the semi-desert fringes of the Sahara, was smaller, a quieter city, but also more important. It was the political capital of the caliphate established a century earlier by the force led by the Islamic scholar Usman dan Fodio. In Sokoto, Caliph Abdurrahman, a descendant of the first caliph, was ailing but determined to resist any advance by the infidel British. Challenged by Lugard to state his position, he wrote to him in uncompromising terms, "I do not consent that any one from you should ever dwell with us," he declared. "I will have nothing ever to do with you. Between us and you there are no dealings except as between Mussulmans and Unbelievers—war."[7]

It was the declaration of war that Lugard needed to justify his next move. Late in January 1903, the necessary soldiers were assembled: 50 officers and around 1,000 men, the largest force yet sent out against a northern state. Setting off from Lokoja once more, the force arrived outside Kano within days. Kano formed an imposing target, surrounded as it was by an unbroken circle of thick walls, 30 feet high and 40 feet wide in places; deep, thorn-filled ditches; and carefully constructed gates. Lugard's wife, the journalist Flora Shaw, later claimed the city could have withstood an "almost interminable" siege had a determined resistance been mounted by its defenders. Once again, it was not. On the first day of the battle, the British cannon punched a hole in the main wall, and, once it was breached, resistance quickly crumbled. "It appeared," the historian Michael Crowder said later, "that the inhabitants . . . were barely concerned about this change of masters."[8] Even the emir's brother, commanding half of Kano's forces, deserted him.

The troops then moved on toward Sokoto, the seat of the century-old caliphate. Caliph Abdurrahman had recently died and been replaced. And after a brief battle, lasting just a few hours, the new caliph, Attahiru Ahmadu, was ousted. He fled, and Sokoto fell. As the north's highest-ranking Islamic leader, Attahiru had some popular support, and when he called on followers to flee, an estimated 25,000 joined him. The British set off in chase and, in a battle a few weeks later, killed Attahiru and scattered his followers.

Triumphant, Lugard arrived in the city four days after the attack, on March 19, and called the city elders to a meeting. The British, he admitted, had not been welcomed by acclamation, but had taken power by force. But this was nothing new, he said. "The Fulani, in old times under dan Fodio, conquered this country. They took the right to rule over it, to levy taxes, to depose kings and to create kings. They in turn have, by defeat, lost their rule . . . All these things which I have said the Fulani by conquest took the right to do, now pass to the British," Lugard declared.[9]

In truth, the battle had not been hard, and, as elsewhere in Nigeria, the firepower of the Maxim gun had not been the decisive factor. More than 20 years earlier in South Africa, a Zulu army equipped with metal spears and cowhide shields had shown, at the battle of Isandlwana, that it was possible for an ill-equipped but determined force to defeat the British army equipped with the most modern weaponry then available. This had not happened in Nigeria.

Like the southern kingdoms before them, the rulers and people of the northern states were neither determined to repulse the British nor united. Years of despotic rule, slave-raiding, and punitive taxes had left the rulers without much popular support, and they had failed to unite among themselves. Like the Yoruba rulers, the northern states were divided and, picked off one by one, they fell. The comparison with the overthrow of the Hausa kings a century earlier was an apt one.

∽

The following year, 1904, the southern governor, Sir Ralph Moor, left Nigeria. Two years later, Lugard left too, trading the challenges of Nigeria for the governorship of Hong Kong. British rule was secure in the north, and he sailed east to Asia, thinking that was that. Consolidating British rule of the tiny colony off southern China, he distinguished his time there by founding the colony's main university and appeared set to remain there for many years to come.

But six years after he left, a financial crisis drew him back to Nigeria. Britain's interest in its giant West African territory had been tempered, from the outset, by concern at its economic cost. Even though trade in the north had picked up since the early years, what Britain earned in taxes and trade from the north was not enough to pay for its administration. In 1910, exports from the south amounted to £4.3 million, while those from the north barely rose above £200,000.[10] This left the north relying on southern subsidies and a sizable grant from London to pay its way, a situation London considered unacceptable. The solution put forward was simple. London would bring the two protectorates together, uniting north and south, bringing them under a joint budget and administration. And Lugard was the man to make it happen.

Returning to Nigeria, Lugard got to work aligning regulations, setting up a new joint customs service, appointing officials, and developing a combined administration. Eighteen months later, on January 1, 1914, he was ready. And with an act of proclamation in London and Lagos, the new nation of Nigeria came into being, north and south as one.

In the manner of its birth, it was an entirely British creation. Since its founding as two separate territories a decade and a half earlier, a series of British businessmen, adventurers, and politicians had determined the existence, the borders, and the political structure of Nigeria. Goldie had drawn a line on the map that decided which parts of what states would comprise the country. He did so ignorant of their histories and traditions. Lugard's wife, Flora Shaw, also a Briton, had created its name, proposing the name Nigeria in her column in *The Times* of London as a play on the name of the great River Niger.[11] The British had even determined the common language Nigerians would speak: English. And they had decided the way they would be ruled. And in all this, Nigerians themselves had barely been consulted, if at all.

For Nigeria to develop properly, this was, of course, the time for nation building to begin, the time for its administrators to think about what they were doing: forcing together two parts of the world with distinct and diverse histories, languages, cultures, and religions. But nation building was not what Lugard had been asked to do.

The sense of unity and national purpose that Nigerians needed would not have made British rule easier. And Lugard opposed anything that might thwart British rule or make it more difficult. Instead, he did what he could to keep the country divided: the north retained its Islamic law traditions and feudal rule while the south adopted English law and welcomed Christian missionaries and education. So while Nigeria was born as one country, one colony, it would not be one nation. The tragedy of Nigeria is that after that first radical act of forging a new country, Britain's governing philosophy was shaped by financial expediency and nervous conservatism, and Nigerians played no real part in it at all.

CHAPTER 5

My Family Connection

*O*n *April 10, 1928,* my grandfather sat writing in his diary in a room at the Euston Hotel in London, readying himself for what lay ahead. Much had changed in Nigeria in the years since Burns had sailed up the coast and Lugard had left. The British had imposed their rule on all parts of the country. New systems of government had been introduced. The British had set up schools, built roads, laid railways, and dredged rivers. To do this, the administration staff had grown. And Hugo Marshall was off to join them.

Born in February 1905 in the village of Limpley Stoke, southern England, Hugo was the sixth of seven children. His father, Henry Marshall, was a city broker who had quit his firm in protest when it invested in one of Leopold's companies in the Congo. His mother was Cecil Mabel Balfour, cousin of the late Edward Burns. Aged nine when World War I started, Hugo had been too young for the conflict that had claimed his elder brother Ernest, a family tragedy that marked him for life. Instead, after school, he studied law at Oxford and then, turned

---

down by the navy because of color blindness, opted for the colonial service instead.

Even then, Nigeria was not the most sought-after foreign posting, unpopular because of the rigors of its climate and the health hazards it posed. But Hugo did not want to work in countries such as Kenya or South Africa. Though he believed in colonial rule, thinking it the best way to promote "development," he did not support the way it was practiced everywhere in Africa. He was critical of the racial policies of South Africa and he opposed the practices of white settlement in Kenya and white rule in East Africa in general.[1] Nigeria was different, he said. In Nigeria, the British ran the government, but Nigerians owned the land. Europeans simply rented it. Britain was the steward, not the owner, of land in Nigeria. It was an important difference. "It is idle to pretend racialism does not exist in Nigeria," he said.[2] But the color bar was not what it was in Kenya or South Africa. That was why he wanted to work there. And, having written up his diary, regretful to be leaving his family and fiancée but excited at the adventure to come, he finished his packing, slept, and set off the next day on the trip to West Africa.

∾

He arrived in Lagos in the middle of a tropical storm. It did not delay him for long. The next day, after signing in at headquarters in Lagos, he was off to the railway yard for a night journey up-country. The railway yard, he said later, was his introduction to Lagos: "A seething mass of carriers, clerks of every description, though all inefficient, of people just back from leave and therefore not too good tempered and, last, but by no means least, a crowd of scoundrels trying to become your servants or trying to get 'dashed'—in either case trying to rob you."

The train on which he traveled north was made up of ten first-class sleepers for the British and four third-class coaches into which the

African passengers were crowded. It left at midnight and arrived in Osogbo around nine o'clock the next morning. From there, he drove on to Akure, the small town in the southwest that was to be his first posting.

Hugo's position was that of a cadet officer, the most junior rung on the colonial ladder available to Europeans. With scant resources at their disposal and a vast territory to control, the British had realized in the days of Lugard that it would be impossible for them to impose their rule directly. They had neither the staff to do so nor the need when there were many Nigerians ready and willing to carry out their orders for them.

What this meant for a junior official such as my grandfather was a role as an overseer of court cases and appeals to traditional rulers. It meant being an administrator of government programs carried out by Nigerian officials. There was too much administration for his liking—taxes and duties to collect, accounts to check, and paperwork to complete. It was "office work," he grumbled. The work he enjoyed was "field research"—sorties into the countryside to get a better understanding of Nigeria.

To a man fresh from legal training, the court work was easy. One day he might hear the case of a woman seeking a divorce on grounds of assault and wounding. Another day, the case might involve petty theft and bribery. Other common cases were land disputes and contract claims. The system adopted in the south where Hugo worked was based, for the most part, on English common law.

His work was not all law, however. At the same time, he had to oversee road-building work and other programs, ordered by the administration in Lagos for his area. Generally, the work found willing volunteers. But where it did not, each town or village the road passed would be asked to contribute labor in lieu of taxes or in return for a modest salary. My grandfather had to see to it that the work was done and sign off on it when the job was completed.

In 1931, he married his childhood sweetheart—my grandmother Susan—and the following year she joined him overseas. When they traveled, they went in colonial style, with porters and a cook, and set up camp in villages and fields. Regular events would be organized at which the British and Nigerian elite would socialize. One year saw my grandparents host a Christmas Day lunch for the alafin of Oyo, one of the most senior Yoruba rulers. Tradition dictated that the alafin could not be seen eating in public, so, around midday, he disappeared into my grandparents' bedroom to consume his lunch in private, leaving a short while later. "A very enjoyable party," my grandfather reported.

There were limits to this fraternization. Life after work for my grandparents was normally a round of drinks and games with other Europeans. He went shooting and played tennis and snooker, the British version of billiards, at a club with friends. She read, painted, and went for walks. When in Lagos they sailed. One of my grandparents' great joint passions was ornithology, and often they went out bird-watching together, he with his gun and she with her notebook and brush. Observing birds from afar, he would try to bring one down. She would paint them while he wrote up the notes. By the time they left the country, they had finished a 14-volume book on Nigerian birds.[3] In all, some 415 species, from the buff-throated sunbird to the blue-breasted kingfisher, fell to her brush and his gun.

His postings took him from Akure to Benin, and from Ibadan to Lagos. And every year, my grandparents, like other officials and their wives, celebrated the King's birthday and Empire Day, events meant to foster respect for the empire, not to promote Nigerian pride. The men donned braided white uniforms and put on pith helmets to give speeches to which, my grandfather suspected, nobody really listened. The audience was too shrewd for that, he would laugh. Duty done, the men changed back into informal attire to lead games and sports, shouting instructions to teams of children, blowing whistles to pick out the winners and losers. It seemed an idyllic life back then.

∾

If idyll it was, it was about to be broken. The year after Hugo arrived, a storm unleashed on Wall Street hit the world and Africa with it. Over the next few years, the Great Depression would cut Nigeria's exports in half, hitting every producer in the pocket and devastating the economy. This had a dramatic effect politically. Nigerians' surprisingly easy acceptance of British rule three decades earlier had been based, in part, on Britain's use of force, in part on Nigerians' disillusionment with their existing rulers, and in part on Britain's promise of development and progress.

Now such progress as had occurred went into reverse. And over the course of the next decade, as the economy tightened, protests grew about everything from taxes to producer prices and labor conditions. For Nigerians and Britons alike, a harsher reality had set in.

In September 1939, a decade after the Depression began, a new world war erupted, a conflict that would cost tens of millions of lives and be waged on every continent, and this affected Nigeria too. First, it sent thousands of young Nigerians overseas to fight in campaigns in India and Burma, witnesses to a type of warfare they had never before seen or imagined. More Nigerians fought in World War II than any other Africans and this had a profound effect on the country when they returned home some years later. Second, the war affected the country economically, and this, in turn, radicalized opinion and put new strains on those responsible for government policy.

For many white officials, the progress of the war became their main concern. From September 1939, my grandfather would go each night to his club in Ibadan, the southwestern town to which he had just been posted, to listen to the news on the wireless. On June 2, 1940, he recorded the events of the day in his diary: "The evacuation from Dunkerque is perfectly marvelous and far surpasses our wildest hopes," he wrote of the escape of Allied forces from northern France. By June 17, the hopes this caused had given way to pessimism: "France is suing for peace. A grim outlook but we shall go on." The war then turned in Britain's favor. The following year, he recorded Germany's attack on Russia and Japan's attack on the United States. "America is in the war now," he wrote. And in 1944, he reported the thrill of D-Day and hopes for Allied victory, though it would take almost another year before it would be declared in Europe and a further three months before the war ended in Asia.

For most Nigerians, the impact of the government's wartime policies was painful. When the war began, London wanted two things above all from its colonies: troops and raw materials. The pressure on the colonies to provide them was immense. Working in Ibadan, my grandfather was told to cut the price paid to farmers for cocoa to force them to produce more palm kernels, then needed as war supplies. He refused. Though he understood the need, he said the proposal was "sweated labor" and would not work in practice. The following year, he rejected demands to cut prices again. The policy of "exploiting the farmers was unpardonable," and he refused to carry it out, he told an official in Lagos.

Workers' strikes and disturbances became more frequent. At the start of the war, there were 12 trade unions in Nigeria. By the war's end, there were 85. Hundreds of days were lost to strike action every year. Often, my grandfather had to mediate between management and workers.

When the war finally came to an end in 1945, it had weakened Europe and ushered in change around the world. In Africa and Asia, the war had eroded belief in the white man's right to rule. The postwar powers, the United States and Russia, opposed colonialism, in theory at least.

And so too did many in the new Labour government elected in London that year.

In Africa and Asia, demands for independence began to grow. In 1947, India gained its freedom after a long campaign led by the Congress Party. In Ghana, the following year, riots broke out. The British officials in the capital, Accra, asked their counterparts in Nigeria for reinforcements. My grandfather, by then based in Lagos, opposed the request. "There is always the danger of the trouble spreading and we are getting too thin on the ground," he wrote.

This should, perhaps, have been the moment when Nigerians rose up to demand their freedom too. But, compared to elsewhere in the world, and elsewhere in Africa too, Nigerians were slow to demand independence.

The first stirrings of an independence movement had emerged in Lagos in the 1920s, when a small clique of lawyers and journalists, men such as the veteran journalist and politician Herbert Macaulay, demanded a say for Africans in the colony's affairs. With little widespread support, such calls were easily bought off with just a few seats handed to Africans on the Lagos town council. In the 1930s, a group called the Nigeria Youth Movement was formed, intent on building a national organization to demand independence. It, too, had limited membership, however. And, moreover, it was soon riven by internal politics and broke up. When politics developed, it did so through three regional, not national, parties. And when this change came, it was, in part at least, at the behest of the British.

In 1946, the British governor of Nigeria, Sir Arthur Richards, was asked by London to draft a fresh constitution for the colony. Ignoring Nigerian voices, he asked my grandfather and other senior colleagues for ideas. What followed was a calamitous decision for Nigeria. Since Lugard's day, the colony had been governed as a country split in two between north and south. The new constitution published in 1947 took this regional structure further. It defined Nigeria not as one but as a federation of three regions—the north unchanged and the south split into east and west—each with its own powerful regional assembly and only a weak central government to hold them all together.

The intent was good, but for those hoping to build Nigeria as one nation, this was more than a setback. The new arrangement set the path for Nigerian independence but failed to forge the unity the country needed. By placing most power in the regions, not in the center, the constitution ensured that the new political parties would develop with a regional, not a national, agenda. To win power, the parties would not need to reach out to voters everywhere. They would have to take power at a regional level and then compete regional party against regional party at the national level. It was a recipe for disaster.

∾

The situation worried my grandfather. In 1952, he was named lieutenant governor of the Western Region, the top official in charge of all of western Nigeria, reporting, along with the lieutenant governors of the eastern and northern regions, to the governor in Lagos. And for his inaugural speech, after inspecting a guard of honor, he chose the topic of trust. Nigerians had suffered hardship because of the Depression and World War II, he said. But things now were improving. Living standards were better than ever, the government was promoting development, and political advances were being made. The problems they faced were surmountable, but only if they could banish the suspicion between the regions that undermined the way the nation worked, he said. However, in the new political setting, one he'd helped create, trust between the regions was hard to find.

Working in Lagos, my grandfather met the new party leaders frequently, the men who would shape Nigeria's early years. One was

Nnamdi Azikiwe, known to all as Zik, a journalist from eastern Nigeria. "Quite decent to talk to, though his paper, *The Pilot,* is scurrilous enough," my grandfather wrote the first time they met. Another was Obafemi Awolowo, a Yoruba journalist and lawyer from the southwest. "Awolowo came up for our first 'heart-to-heart' chat. At first he was rather cagey but he gradually thawed. He is complex . . . a difficult character," Hugo wrote. The third was Ahmadu Bello, an aristocrat, a descendant of Usman dan Fodio, and the champion of the north, who came to dinner when in Lagos. "Very reserved," was my grandfather's initial thought on meeting him. Their first dinner was "rather heavy weather."

My grandfather's relationship with the Yoruba leader Awolowo was initially difficult and strained. Superficially relations appeared good. When my mother and her brothers were on a visit to Nigeria in 1952, Awolowo would bring his children to the house to play with them while the adults talked indoors. Often they would meet for dinner and attend official functions together, socializing with their wives. But first, Awolowo, a man in his own country, was determined to wrest power away from my grandfather, the white official. And soon he devised a way to test how far he could push him.

At a cabinet meeting in June 1952, the two men disputed the procedure for naming officials to a new government agency set up in the Western Region. My grandfather thought the final word should be his. Awolowo could suggest any name he wanted but my grandfather would decide. On paper he was right. That was the law. But politics was changing things. And Awolowo was outraged when told that, even as the newly elected regional prime minister, he still had to seek the approval of the senior British official to make appointments to his administration. He liked my grandfather, a man he called "a highly seasoned and experienced administrator." But he said he had not been elected leader of the Western Region "merely to reinforce his team of official advisers." He and his allies had been elected "to govern the region according to our own light," Awolowo said.[4]

When my grandfather refused to cede ground, Awolowo announced a boycott of all further official meetings until the dispute was resolved. The two sides went to Lagos for talks with the governor, and Awolowo was unrelenting. "Awful," my grandfather wrote privately that night. "It went on for hours." It was my grandfather's nerve that broke first. "Finished at 7:30. Exhausted. Dinner after which I was physically sick. Early to bed," he wrote that night.

∾

The political leaders in the south were now pushing hard for independence. The world had indeed changed with the end of World War II. With freedom granted to India, and moves to self-rule under way around Africa, it was clear that, in Nigeria too, colonial rule would soon have had its day. The British wanted out. They were happy to go, but wanted the timetable to be agreed upon by all the regional leaders, not just those from the south. And that was the problem. Because, with things as they stood, the north did not want independence to come too soon.

In March 1953, one of Obafemi Awolowo's MPs, Anthony Enahoro, made a speech in the assembly demanding that a date be set for self-government. The proposal caused an uproar, not among the British, but among the northern MPs. Since Lugard's fateful decision, in the first years of colonial rule, to keep northern Nigeria separate from the rest, development there had lagged behind that in the south. With fewer schools and colleges in the north, many posts in the northern administration had had to be filled by southerners. As independence approached, the situation alarmed northern politicians, who feared that if self-rule came too soon, the north would be dominated not by the British but by southern officials now working under the British. And that, unlike the British, these men would use their power at the north's expense.

"The south is moving too fast," northern leaders such as Ahmadu Bello said. The southern politicians attacked the northern leaders in return. My grandfather, watching in parliament, was alarmed. "Very strong views were expressed by the north . . . The dangers to Nigeria are very real and serious . . . trouble lies ahead," he wrote the night after parliament broke up. My grandfather organized a series of dinners trying to get Awolowo, Azikiwe, and Bello to talk to one another. They each came, but always separately, never all three together. A few days after Enahoro's speech, Awolowo returned to the attack, making what my grandfather thought an "un-prepared and ill-advised" speech. "He attacked the north and, worse, taunted the north," my grandfather wrote. Driving home from Lagos after parliament concluded its session, the cars carrying northern members of parliament were pelted with stones, and northern leaders were jeered on the streets. A few weeks later, anti-southern riots broke out in Kano when Awolowo visited. "The strains in the country are very real," my grandfather wrote.

The next year, 1954, my grandfather flew to London for talks in Cumberland House, presided over by the secretary of state for the colonies and attended by Nigerian leaders and British officials. A timetable for independence was finally agreed on. Calls for separate regional assemblies for the Mid-West, the Niger Delta, and the Middle Belt, to break up the power of the big three regions, were brushed aside. So were calls for a strong government at the center and other constitutional proposals aimed at averting regional tensions. The three regions could apply for self-government beginning in 1956, the conference agreed. They would have to do so by 1959. The British would be out by 1960. As Nigeria prepared for independence, more elections were organized, the results dominated, predictably, by the three big regional parties. Nothing in the constitution could force them to work together. The north was still uneasy about independence but was kept onboard by a British promise to organize, even to fix, the elections in a way to ensure it would hold majority power in the new parliament. The politicians from the south were unhappy with this but accepted it as the price to pay for independence.

And, in all this time, there was scarcely a strong, popular voice heard. All the pressure for independence had come from officials and politicians.

∽

All over Africa, the British were leaving, scrambling to get out of the continent that they had fought to claim as their own half a century earlier. Sudan was the first to achieve independence, in 1956, and Ghana a year later, in 1957. In the year Nigeria would become independent, 1960, 17 African nations would be given their freedom.

With the timetable for independence agreed on, my grandparents left Nigeria in 1955. The last few years had been draining for both of them. My grandfather was an able administrator, but he was no politician, and he'd found little pleasure in governing for the last few years. After his confrontation with Awolowo, he had thought of resigning but had been persuaded against it. In 1954, he was made chief secretary of the colony in Lagos and served for two months as acting governor when the governor was on leave. And then, in 1955, having turned 50 and spent so much of his lifetime living abroad, he decided to return to England and family. With power transferring to the Nigerian politicians, he had little left to do in Nigeria, he said.

On August 2, 1955, more than 27 years after he arrived in Lagos for the first time, it was time to leave. My grandparents held a last dinner for friends and officials. And then at nine o'clock the next morning, the council of ministers came down to the jetty to see them off. At the harbor, they were given a guard of honor and said goodbye to friends, some of whom they had known for almost 30 years. Some were dignitaries. Others were members of their household staff. As they left, Buramoh, a man who had served them as house steward for a quarter of a century, broke down and wept. The police buglers sounded a farewell. The Yacht Club, with which they had sailed for a decade, sounded a signal. They waved to those ashore, and they crossed the harbor for the last time, to join the ship to take them home.

∾

With five years still to go before independence, my grandfather left Nigeria unsatisfied with what he had achieved. Three regional parties had been brought into being. Three skilled but flawed politicians had been placed on the national stage. And too little had been done to prepare the people for rule by elected government. Few understood how the new government was supposed to work. My grandfather was leaving, he believed, with a job unfinished.

"For those who understood what was happening, independence was a time of hope, yes. But also one of fear," Harold Dappe-Biriye, a delta politician, told me many years later.[5]

The country appeared stable, and the economy was growing. But, as leader of the delta's Itsekiri people, he "knew that independence on the ticket of three tribes would lead to trouble and conflict and subject the minorities to oppression, and it did."

The constitutional structure created by the British, by my grandfather and his colleagues in 1947, had set the regions against one another. This was not their intent, but it was the outcome. It was not the stable platform the country needed. And whatever their hope and pride at independence, many Nigerians besides Dappe-Biriye feared what would happen as a result and did so with good reason.

However, with history calling, such concerns were brushed aside. At midnight on October 1, 1960, the new federal prime minister, a northern politician called Abubakar Tafawa Balewa, stepped up to a microphone at the central square in Lagos and declared Nigeria free. "The great day" had arrived, he stated. After lengthy negotiations with the British, independence had come. The country was free and stood "well-built on firm foundations." All over the country, people celebrated. Parades were held, and fireworks were launched into the sky. From his official residence in Kaduna, the Northern Region premier, Ahmadu Bello, declared himself "most happy and proud" at the achievement.[6] Hundreds of miles to the south, Obafemi Awolowo, the leader of the Yoruba, celebrated too.

Back in England, my grandfather pondered what the outcome would be. It wasn't long before the country provided an answer. And when it came, it wasn't a happy one.

CHAPTER 6

Civil War
and Bloodshed

For reporters of my generation, the conflict that broke out in Yugoslavia in the 1990s was the defining news event of the decade. I was a junior reporter on my agency's Paris news desk at the time, and Yugoslavia was my first major foreign assignment. For many journalists of an earlier generation, however, the defining conflict was Biafra, the civil war that erupted five years after Nigerian independence, raged for two and a half years, and left up to 1 million dead and millions more homeless.[1]

The coup that broke Nigeria got under way in the early hours of a Saturday morning, just after 2 A.M. on a January day in 1966. Gravel crunched underfoot. If anyone had stirred at the noise and looked at their clock, they would have rolled over and gone back to sleep. Then, over the night sounds of cicadas scratching and lizards scuttling, came a whispering, followed by the thump of a boot and the splintering of wood as a door was kicked in. After overpowering the police guards, Major Emmanuel Ifeajuna, an athlete who had starred at the Empire

---

Games in Canada more than a decade earlier, was making for the prime minister's quarters.[2]

Just a few days earlier, Nigeria had played host to dozens of world leaders. Well liked by many, Prime Minister Abubakar Tafawa Balewa had won plaudits for his staging of the first Commonwealth Conference ever held outside London. Since independence in 1960, the country had been ruled by Tafawa Balewa's northern-based party, the Northern People's Congress (NPC). And it had known its share of troubles. Elections held after independence had been heavily rigged. There had been trouble in the southwest. Corruption was widespread and growing. But, set against the problems seen elsewhere, these were seen by many outside Nigeria as "teething troubles." The most populous country in Africa was fulfilling its promise as a strong, stable, independent nation, *The Times* of London declared in an editorial.[3] But this rosy view of affairs would all change with the coup.

If they'd been happy at independence, the army and the population were now simmering with discontent. Led by Major Ifeajuna, the soldiers who burst in on the sleeping prime minister were angry. The hope that had been so palpable at independence had evaporated in five short years. In that time, the economy had grown steadily, with average real incomes rising by 5 percent per year. But election-related violence had unsettled the country and corruption had tarnished the reputation of all politicians. Opposition candidates had seen their meetings disrupted. Politicians had been attacked by rivals hoping to intimidate them and their voters. In the worst incidents, gangs on either side had hunted down their opponents, doused them in petrol, and burned them alive—in what became known as "Operation Weti-e!" (literally, "douse it"). And relations between the regions were dire. It was into this situation that the coup plotters stepped.

Waking Tafawa Balewa, Ifeajuna allowed the prime minister to say his prayers, then led him away and bundled him into a car, ignoring the protestations of his wife. The soldiers then went next door and detained Festus Okotie-Eboh, the finance minister, known for his corruption and high living, and forced him into a car too.

Around town, other units went in search of the army chief of staff, quartermaster general, and adjutant general—men who might support the government. Machine-gunned down in their homes near the city's Apapa port, their bodies were thrown into a waiting truck. Ifeajuna himself drove out of Lagos with the prime minister in the back of his car. When he reached the outskirts, he ordered Tafawa Balewa out, shot him dead, and dumped his body into a ditch. The finance minister was shot dead nearby.

In Ibadan, the capital of the troubled Western Region, the target was Samuel Akintola, the regional premier and an ally of Tafawa Balewa. The guards outside his residence were easily overpowered by the rebels. But, alerted by a phone call from his deputy's wife, Akintola barricaded himself indoors, armed with a submachine gun. When the soldiers approached, he waited until they were just outside, then fired through the closed door. When he ran out of bullets, he surrendered and was shot dead.

In Kaduna, the capital of the north, the target was Ahmadu Bello, premier of the north. After crossing the city, the leaders of the coup shot their way into his grounds and set his house ablaze. When a guard rushed out wielding a sword, he was disarmed, and the rebel soldiers rushed inside. As they pushed past crying women and children, they forced their way into Bello's private rooms, put him up against a wall, and shot him dead. His senior wife and a bodyguard died with him. Other senior military officials in the town were also killed.

In Lagos, the instigators of the coup, a small group of middle-ranking army majors from eastern Nigeria, had succeeded in capturing or killing most of their targets, but a few had escaped. One of them was the future military ruler and war leader Lieutenant Colonel Yakubu "Jack"

Gowon, tipped off, it is said, by his Igbo girlfriend. Others included one of the army's most senior commanders, and the future military ruler, Major General Johnson Aguyi-Ironsi. When Aguyi-Ironsi realized what was happening, he rallied loyal troops from the town's Ikeja barracks and confronted the rebel soldiers. Surrounded and outnumbered, the rebels quickly surrendered.

In Kaduna, the leader of the coup in the north went on local radio declaring it still alive despite what had happened in Lagos. The coup leaders were aiming to establish a "strong, united and prosperous nation, free from corruption and internal strife," Major Chukwuma Nzeogwu said. The enemies of their new Revolutionary Council were the people who had hurt Nigeria, he said: "the political profiteers, the swindlers, the men in high and low places that seek bribes, the tribalists, the nepotists."[4] But with Lagos back in the hands of army loyalists, it was bluster. And two days later, he too surrendered.

Across the south, many people celebrated the end of the government, even if they disapproved of so much shedding of blood. Since 1960, the government led by Tafawa Balewa had followed an overt policy of "northernization," diverting federal resources to the region and systematically favoring northern candidates for jobs and contracts in a bid to help it to catch up with the south.

So southerners celebrated its demise. Students at the university in Ibadan erupted with joy at the news, embracing, hugging, drumming, drinking, and dancing.[5] Supporters of the Yoruba leader Obafemi Awolowo issued a statement cheering the killing of Samuel Akintola, who had allied himself with Tafawa Balewa. "The day of January 15 will pass into the history of our great republic as the day when we achieved true liberty . . . We salute the new regime," Awolowo's allies said.[6]

But in the north, the coup was seen as a tribal takeover by Igbos of the north. For all that Nzeogwu decried the "tribalists" in government, the leading victims of the coup were all northerners or their allies, northern leaders noted, and all the coup leaders but one were Igbos, men from the southeast. And, what is more, the man the coup would bring to power, Major General Aguyi-Ironsi, was Igbo too.

In his home in southern England, my grandfather was aghast. Tuning in on the radio, he was appalled to hear what had happened. Coups had taken place in a dozen other countries over the previous few years, but it was a "crushing disappointment" that it would happen in Nigeria, he told a friend. Though he thought little of some of those who had been killed, he was an admirer of Abubakar Tafawa Balewa, who he thought had been a moderating figure in the northern government. "Abubakar is a terrible loss to Africa," he said when the late prime minister's death was confirmed.

∼

Once the bloodshed stopped, Nigerians gathered in workplaces and on street corners to discuss what had happened. Two things had. Both were alarming. First, the coup had put an end to civilian rule for a generation. Terrified by what had happened to Tafawa Balewa and his colleagues, the surviving members of the government had asked the head of the army, Major General Aguyi-Ironsi, to take "interim" power, and he now agreed. Few thought the arrangement would be short-lived.

Second, the coup had brought Nigeria's deep-seated regional rivalries out into politics as never before. Whether or not what had happened was, in fact, an Igbo coup, organized to an eastern agenda, that was how it was perceived in the north and that was what mattered. The coup played to old northern fears of domination by the Igbos, fears that went back to the days before independence. And combined with army anger at what had happened in the coup, these fears would soon lead the north to strike back.

The north's fears of Igbo rule were already at fever pitch when Aguyi-Ironsi was named in January as military ruler. They seemed confirmed in May when the new ruler signed a decree replacing the regional system of government with a system of strong central government. Aguyi-Ironsi's goal was an end to "regionalism," he and his supporters said. If so, what northerners saw was a government dominated by Igbos from Aguyi-Ironsi down.

On the streets of northern towns and cities, ordinary northerners vented their anger by unleashing attacks on Igbos and other easterners. In a wave of killings following the announcement, easterners living in the north were dragged from their shops and homes and killed on the streets. The scale of the bloodshed was shocking. For six weeks, killings occurred every day. Tens of thousands died. And as the violence continued, trainloads of Igbos fled the region, heading east, bringing with them gruesome evidence of the attacks they had suffered: machete wounds, knife wounds, and stories of rapes and murders. Some women reputedly returned east carrying the severed heads of slaughtered sons and husbands in their pitiful possessions, unable, in their grief, to let go.

In Lagos, a badly ruffled Aguyi-Ironsi recognized the need to calm tempers and set off on a fence-mending tour of the nation, but it was too late. Northern elements in the army had already decided to act. At the end of July, a northern countercoup took place. On a visit to Ibadan, in the southwest, Aguyi-Ironsi was abducted from a government building, taken to a forest outside the city, tortured, and killed. Others linked to him were similarly slaughtered. The operation unleashed was codenamed Araba, the Hausa word for secession.

Though secession of the north was the initial plan, the coup leaders, including the future military ruler Brigadier Murtala Muhammed, were soon persuaded to think again. British and American diplomats held hurried talks with the country's new leaders to explain that, with

Aguyi-Ironsi dead, the north was now in a position to dictate affairs. Should they cut themselves off from the south, the north would face a poorer and more uncertain future than if they stayed, they were told, and they agreed. Stay they did. And so began almost three decades of northern military rule.

To calm southern fears about the new regime, the man chosen as the new head of state was not from the far north, nor was he a Muslim. He was a Christian from the central region known as the Middle Belt. Aged only 31 at the time he took power, Lieutenant Colonel Yakubu "Jack" Gowon was one of the young officers who had survived the first coup after a tip-off from his Igbo girlfriend. The fresh-faced son of two church workers, he was popular with colleagues and not considered a political schemer. He would lead Nigeria for the next nine years.

And Gowon's first step after taking power was to call a constitutional conference to find a way for Nigerians to live together. Even after the tumult of the second coup had died down, it appeared that Nigeria could not last as one country, so bitter were relations now, but Gowon said he was determined to try.

As the conference began in September, delegates from the north and east railed at each other while events on the ground were pushing the country further apart. The mass killings of May resumed that month with northern mobs setting upon Igbos in the streets and hunting them down in their homes, not only in the north but in major southern cities such as Lagos too. Thousands more were killed. To the Igbos, it was genocide.

∾

The two men who now emerged as the two key figures in the nation's life were Gowon, in Lagos, and his rival in the east, Lieutenant Colonel Emeka Ojukwu.

Superficially, their life stories bore some similarities. Both had been born in central Nigeria and had joined the army and attended the British military academy at Sandhurst together. The two men knew each other well. But there, the similarities ended. Where Gowon was the modest son of church workers from a minority ethnic group and largely uninvolved in politics up to the time of his nomination as head of state, Ojukwu was the confident child of Nigeria's first multimillionaire, Sir Louis Ojukwu, the first president of African Continental Bank and the Nigerian Stock Exchange, born into money and privilege, able, intelligent, and ambitious. Unlike Gowon, Ojukwu had been educated at private school in England before attending Oxford, where he studied history, and had both a broad worldview and the certainty of attitude that often goes with an Oxford education. So, when the July coup took place and the position of Igbos in Nigeria seemed under the gravest threat, Ojukwu was the man they turned to. And when they did so, he declared that the east would not recognize Gowon as its leader.

In the first week of January 1967, with the fate of Nigeria in their hands, the two men agreed to meet. Unwilling to do so in Nigeria, Gowon and Ojukwu flew to Ghana for talks on their country's future. Two days later, they left, both apparently believing they had a deal, a solution that broke up Nigeria in all but name but avoided bloodshed. But once they got home, the agreement fell apart. Though tape recordings of the talks produced later by Ojukwu showed what had been agreed, no papers had been signed at the meeting and Gowon backtracked. For Ojukwu, this was the final straw.

Following the months of killings in the north and in Lagos, Ojukwu was clear that the east could not remain part of Nigeria. And since the north had rejected his demand for secession, war beckoned. So be it. The east built up its forces and, on May 26, 1967, the Eastern

Region assembly met and authorized Ojukwu to declare independence from Nigeria. And at dawn on May 30, 1967, he proclaimed the secession of the east and the birth of what he named the Republic of Biafra.

~

For six weeks, the country simmered. Then, in July, Gowon struck. He launched what he called a "police action" to end the east's rebellion. The position of the federals, as the Nigerian side became known, was a simple one. Nigeria could and indeed must remain one nation. Plastered onto billboards and aired on the radio, federal slogans called for unity. "To Keep Nigeria One, Is a Task That Must Be Done," said the best known. There were many reasons given. The most compelling was that to allow the secession of Biafra would be to invite the breakup not just of Nigeria but of countless other countries across Africa, threatening bloodshed on a terrifying scale. Another reason, not often aired in public, was oil.

Though oil was not the cause of the Biafra war, it was indisputably a factor. Discovered in the Niger Delta in 1956, just four years before independence, oil was vital to the economic future of the region. And the territory declared independent by Ojukwu comprised not just traditional Igbo areas but much of the delta too, including its main oil-producing areas. Oil gave both sides something extra to fight for.

From the outset in May 1967, it looked like a one-sided war. The federal side had 40,000 men under arms, with many more in reserve, and Ojukwu had just 25,000. Beginning their attack in July, the federal forces quickly took a lot of ground. One of the first places to fall was Nsukka, a small university town just north of Enugu. But the progress of the federals was slow. The federal forces were powerful but disorganized, and Biafran resistance was stiffer than expected. Scarred by the massacres of Igbos in the north and west, most Igbos believed the fre-quent warnings from Ojukwu that, if defeated, they faced genocide, and fought hard. And, in early August, the Biafrans struck back.

Breaking out of their eastern enclave, Biafran forces crossed the Niger and surged westward toward Lagos. Seizing a series of midsized towns in 12 days, they pushed on to within 100 miles of the capital. The rapid advance threw Lagos into panic. But the rebel forces had over-stretched. They paused, and their next push through the lagoon toward Lagos was repulsed at Okitipupa, a small town east of Lagos, at the east-ern end of the lagoon. The federal side regrouped and, at the end of the month, forced the Biafrans into retreat. As the year ended, the federals had again captured more than half of Biafran territory. They had Enugu, Bonny, and Calabar under their control. Onitsha and Port Harcourt fol-lowed by April the next year.

If anyone's intent had been to save lives, it was then that the war should have ended. Had it done so, much suffering and misery would have been avoided. But, with victory seemingly certain, the federal side would not give up now. And Ojukwu himself was not a man to con-template surrender. Proud and contemptuous of "young Jack Gowon," he refused point-blank to consider defeat an option.

Over the coming year, the war settled into a pattern, with dogged defense of towns and fields by the Biafrans and inept offensives by the federal side. Both sides used conscripts as well as volunteers and made targets of civilians. Federal and Biafran air raids spread death and terror from the sky, while ground troops brought the conflict to street level. In one of the finer novels of the period, *Sozaboy: A Novel in Rotten English,* Ken Saro-Wiwa, who as an Ogoni from the delta supported the feder-als, tells the story of a naïve young recruit who was proud to fight at the outset of the war but quickly became disillusioned. "The war have spoiled my town Dukana, uselessed many people, killed many others, killed my mama and my wife, Agnes . . . Now, if anybody say anything about war or even fight, I will just run and run and run," the character says.[7] And many agreed.

For month after month, the Igbos held out against the attacks, testing their ingenuity and resilience to the limit. But slowly and surely, the territory they controlled shrank. Squeezed in on all sides, people became refugees in their own land, crowded into an area one-tenth the size of the original Biafra, in scenes vividly captured in Chimamanda Adichie's civil war novel *Half of a Yellow Sun*.

And then, in December 1969, two and a half years after it all began, the final campaign began that would end the war once and for all. Led by the future military ruler Colonel Olusegun Obasanjo, the 3rd Marine Commando Division made a strong push up into Biafra from the south to end Biafran resistance. When the last major town of Owerri fell to the federals on January 8, 1970, it was obvious to all that the end was close, and three days later, in the early hours of January 11, Ojukwu finally fled Biafra, flying on the last plane out of Uli, an improvised airstrip the Biafrans had used to bring in aid.

The following day, Ojukwu's deputy, Major General Philip Effiong, took to the radio and admitted defeat. "I am convinced now that a stop must be put to the bloodshed which is going on as a result of the war," he declared. Ojukwu had been the main obstacle to peace, but now he was gone. "Our people are now disillusioned and those elements of the old government regime who have made negotiations and reconciliation impossible have voluntarily removed themselves from our midst," Effiong said.[8]

The following day, Effiong was brought to Lagos for a formal surrender to Gowon. By then, the war had cost up to 1 million lives, most of them Biafran. Many had died slowly and painfully, of starvation and disease. There had been thousands of incidents of rape, random killings, looting, and much suffering. In a first for the world, harrowing scenes of stick-thin children with distended bellies were shown on TV screens worldwide; this was the first African war to shock the globe.

ॐ

Thirty years later to the day, I walked up the path to a modest, white-walled house in the former Eastern Region capital of Enugu to meet the man who, in fighting Gowon, had started the war. Pardoned in 1982 for his role in the conflict, Ojukwu had been allowed to return from self-imposed exile and had settled back at home in the east. To his supporters, disillusioned with the place given to Igbos in postwar Nigeria, Ojukwu was still a hero and president of the state of Biafra, a state for which some continued to yearn and still do.

How should I address him? I wondered. Ojukwu is a proud man, I had been told. I asked the aide who answered the door.

"You can call him 'His Excellency' or 'Mr. President,'" the aide replied. Ojukwu might have led a rebellion that ended in defeat three decades earlier. But, to his supporters, he was still the leader of Biafra and the war was not quite over.

"He was the President, you know."

Like many a big man's house in Nigeria, the main room of his home was decked out with thronelike chairs and giant photographs of the owner and their family. When Ojukwu entered, I expected to be awed by his presence. But when the door opened, he came in barefoot, tall and well-built but wearing a simple flowing white robe, almost humble. He had the same striking eyes, balding forehead, and neatly trimmed beard I had seen in war photos. But the beard was flecked now with gray and the eyes were sad. "No need to stand on ceremony," he said, gesturing for me to sit. His voice was deep and low, mellifluous, Oxford-accented, warm.

I explained why I was there: the thirtieth anniversary of the end of the war. He stayed silent. Looking back three decades, did he regret the conflict? I asked. His eyes flickered as though a switch had been turned.

"The war was a tragedy," he rumbled, "but it was inevitable, unavoidable." It was not a conflict he had sought. Nobody wanted war, least of all those who knew what it meant to fight. "But the Igbos had no choice. It was a fight for the survival of the Igbo people against plans to wipe out a generation. That was the issue that we faced: genocide."

We moved on. We discussed the course of the conflict, the role of the West, of Britain and France. And we talked about the point, in 1968, when hope seemed lost. Wasn't that the time to consider surrender? I asked. When it was clear that Biafra could not win, should he not have ordered a surrender sooner, to save lives? Should the war have ended two years earlier than it had?

"No, of course not," Ojukwu shot back, leaning forward now in his chair, gripping the armrest. "How many people in world history, in Western civilization, have surrendered just because they were hungry? You fight on as long as you can. We fought proudly for as long as we could," he said.

But his people, the people who had sought secession and fought the war, had not been simply hungry, I replied. Young and old, they had succumbed, fighting on, to starvation and disease. Was it pride, then, that had kept them going? Was it his pride?

"It was not *my* pride. They fought proudly, *we* fought proudly, as a proud people should," Ojukwu answered, his voice rising in outrage.

With his departure, Biafra had collapsed, and yet, there had been no genocide. Did that not suggest the Igbos had been wrong to fight? They had not faced genocide, had they? Did he feel any hint of responsibility for starting, and prolonging, the war?

"No, none at all," he boomed, affronted at the thought. "It was clear from the massacres we faced genocide. It was fighting on that convinced them they could not carry it out. I see the outcome of the war as a fulfillment of our war aims. We survived," he said.

And what of the position of the Igbos in Nigeria today? "The position of the Igbos in Nigeria is a regret," he agreed. "We are marginalized in Nigeria. You will never find an Igbo man at the highest level. That is the problem of Nigeria."

Ojukwu is a historic figure, I thought, and a complex one. He fought for the Igbos' right to self-rule. He was outraged at what had happened to the Igbos in Nigeria. He sacrificed. But pride and obstinacy had blinded him to his chance to save lives when he could. And it had gotten in the way of clear judgment then and now. Old divisions remained. Hundreds of thousands had died because of it.

We talked some more, and then, suddenly, the interview was over. Ojukwu had had a call to go to a meeting. He looked tired, and his voice had gone flat, but he would summon himself up again. We stood, and I asked if I could take a photo of him. He agreed, but then hesitated. Pride intervened. "You can, but don't show my feet," he asked. I didn't understand. "Don't show that I am barefoot. It is not very dignified," he said. I obliged. I shook his hand. And, with that, the president left the room.

CHAPTER 7

Misrule and Plunder

*I*n *a speech delivered* in the midst of a torrential Lagos downpour, nine months after the war ended, General Gowon set out his government's plans. With the fighting over, he promised peace and reconciliation. The war, he said, had been 30 months of "a grim struggle," 30 months of "sacrifice and national agony." The federal cause had been just. Now it was time for "reconciliation, reconstruction, and rehabilitation."[1] On the tenth anniversary of independence, it was time to look ahead, to rebuild and develop the economy, reshape the constitution, and, when all was in place, return power to the people. To do all this would take time—six years, he said—to return Nigeria to a system of civilian rule. But, like the war, it was a "Task that Must be Done."

Fresh from victory, the chance Gowon had now was to build a united nation, the first real opportunity given to any Nigerian leader since the country's founding in 1900. And based on the ideals he espoused of unity and progress, Nigeria should indeed have prospered, rich as it was in land, timber, fisheries, tin, coal, gold, oil, and gas, with a civil

service then admired by many and a population among the most educated in the developing world.

But Gowon, a steady war leader, would prove hopeless as president,
failing to plan, to control army corruption, or to develop the economy
as promised. And in 1974, he admitted that he would miss his own dead-
line to end army rule too.

And what followed, in July 1975, was another coup (the country's
third), followed by four more years of military rule, a brief civilian
regime, and the return of the military. Nigerians witnessed corruption
in government and stagnation in the economy, an oil boom followed by
an oil bust, people flocking to the cities, and, in the next decades, three
further coups, each one inspiring less hope than the last. And with each
passing coup, the cause of this instability was less the errors of the constitution drawn up for independence and more the lure of oil, and the
way the new rulers were allowed to get away, scot-free, with misrule and
corruption.

∾

The soldier who replaced Gowon in July 1975 was Brigadier Murtala
Muhammed, the man behind the northern "countercoup" staged nine
years earlier. This time, the coup was bloodless. Gowon, whose popularity
was low, was abroad when the coup took place and was unharmed.
Muhammed, the new ruler, produced a flurry of action to fight inflation,
strengthen the economy, and crack down on corruption. Every month,
he launched a new initiative, and this approach, and the firm manner
with which he ruled, won Muhammed popularity at home.

But, though he was popular with the people at large, Muhammed
had still come to power in a coup, and this meant he had enemies. Lieutenant Colonel Bukar Dimka was one. Coming from the Middle Belt,
and related by marriage to Gowon, he had not accepted what had hap-

pened that year and went to see Gowon, then studying politics at a university in England. What was discussed is unknown. But a few weeks later, on the morning of February 13, 1976, when Muhammed was driving to work, Dimka struck. As Muhammed's chauffeur drove him through the streets of Lagos, a small group of soldiers led by Dimka sprayed the general's car with bullets. Muhammed, his aide-de-camp, an orderly, and the driver were all killed. The shell of the bullet-ridden car can be seen today in Lagos's National Museum.

After killing Muhammed, Dimka seized a radio station to announce to the nation what had happened and call for a change of regime. When he did so, he had little support and, within hours, he had fled. Muhammed's number two, Olusegun Obasanjo, was named in his place and vowed to pursue his former boss's policies and his program for returning the nation to civilian rule.

Under the Obasanjo regime, the role of the state in the economy grew, and Nigeria took a more assertive, pan-Africanist stance, remained critical of the West, and declared itself a staunch opponent of apartheid South Africa. Spending rose as oil prices pushed government revenue higher. Much was wasted, but some much-needed roads and hospitals were built. And then, as promised, the army staged elections to usher in a return to civilian rule.

The new constitution, brought in by the military, made some sensible changes to the constitution agreed to by the British. It required political parties to open offices in each of the then 19 states, and seek support there. And it required presidential candidates to achieve at least 25 percent support in at least two-thirds of the states to win. The new politics would be national, not regional, the army had declared.

But still, the military did not give the parties free rein to organize as they pleased. Fearful of being held to account for its misrule of past years, the military required all parties to register and banned all those that it feared might have a radical agenda. And the parties that were allowed to run still had little real grassroots support.

∾

Shehu Shagari, the former schoolteacher elected president in 1979, was ill-suited to the role he was elected to. Weak and indecisive, he was the puppet of the party that put him into power and was elected without a strong personal or policy mandate. With such disadvantages, it was no surprise that he failed.

During the oil-boom years of the mid-1970s, Nigerians' average income had grown, but the income had been skewed very unevenly in favor of the new oil elite, and much state income had been squandered. Agriculture and manufacturing had declined. When oil prices crashed in the 1980s, the now oil-dependent economy collapsed with them. Public services disintegrated, and public sector workers launched a wave of strikes. After four years of drift and decline, Nigerians had seen enough of Shagari. But the 1983 elections were rigged, and Shagari returned to power, though not for long.

The country's fourth coup took place on the last day of the year in 1983. Again, it was no popular revolt, just a changing of the guard. The president, vice president, and a host of other leaders were arrested, to the usual popular cheers. The army was back. And again, the new rulers denounced the old, without promising any real change.

The new head of state was General Muhammadu Buhari, an austere figure with a reputation as a disciplinarian, and not known as personally corrupt. "Our economy has been hopelessly mismanaged," announced his then spokesman, Colonel Sani Abacha, who would become a military ruler himself one day. "We have become a debtor and beggarly nation . . . Health services are in a shambles . . . Our education system is deteriorating at an alarming rate," said Abacha, who would make them even worse one day. "Unemployment figures have reached embarrassing and unacceptable proportions," he said. The military had seized power to restore proper order. "This government will not tolerate kickbacks, inflation of contracts and over-invoicing of imports . . . nor will it condone forgery, fraud, embezzlement . . . and smuggling," Abacha unblushingly declared.[2]

Buhari's first real act as ruler was to launch what he called his "War against Indiscipline," arresting hundreds of leading politicians and civil servants for corruption and announcing a series of new offenses from jaywalking to spitting in the streets to restore order in daily life. For more serious crimes, such as drug-running, Buhari ordered public executions, some carried out on a popular Lagos beach. But he did not know how to rebuild the economy, and his tough stance on crime lost him support. So 20 months later, with the economy still in decline, it was no surprise to Nigerians to turn on their radios and hear the martial music and gravelly-voiced announcement of Nigeria's fifth coup since independence.

∾

Ibrahim Babangida, the new head of state, was in power from 1985 to 1993 and is perhaps the most intriguing figure to have led Nigeria since independence. He was certainly the most politically skilled. Born in Minna, northern Nigeria, in 1941, Babangida was a career officer and serial plotter with a hand in almost every coup since the northern coup of 1966. After finally coming to power in 1985, his big ambition was to do what his civilian and military predecessors had failed to do and take the steps needed to turn the economy around. The way he tried to do this and dodge the political blame for any financial pain earned him the nickname the "Maradona of Nigerian Politics" from the awed Nigerian press, his silky presentational skills calling to mind the deft touch of the Argentine soccer player.

From the start, Babangida had a better understanding of economics than his predecessors. And, unlike Muhammed and Obasanjo, he was a free-market liberal, keen to shrink the role of the state and pursue a more open economy. To do this, Babangida brought in good advisers and did as they suggested, selling off state firms, letting the currency reach its market level, relaxing rules, and liberalizing import controls. After a long slide, the economy started slowly to turn around.

But the reforms were slow to show results that would please ordinary people. The withdrawal of state subsidies and cuts in public payrolls, demanded by the country's creditors, were unpopular on the streets. Protests on student campuses began and, when these coincided with two fresh coup attempts, Babangida lost his nerve, abandoned the reforms, and clamped down. He knew better than most that an unpopular ruler was more vulnerable to another coup than a popular one. So Babangida turned to a second strategy to maintain his power, siphoning millions, even billions, of dollars from the public purse to channel to his family, his cronies, and his supporters nationwide. And for those unwilling to take the money, he turned to suppression. Student groups were shut down. Journalists were locked up or killed. Trade unions were taken over or closed.

In 1990, in time-honored tradition, Babangida announced plans to hand over power once the political framework to do so could be put in place. No new constitution was needed. What was required, he said, was a "new breed" of politicians.

First, he brought together political allies to create two parties, one center-right, the other center-left, to run for office in elections to be conducted by the military. How the parties could represent the will of the people if they were created by the military was unclear. The elections went ahead, however, and in June 1993 millions turned out to vote in the presidential round. But, when the elections ended, it became clear

that the southern candidate, a Yoruba businessman called Moshood Abiola, who Babangida had thought would lose, had in fact won. Babangida,
the master of Nigerian politics, had got it wrong.

In Abiola's strongholds, riots broke out. Babangida's army rivals saw
their chance to oust him. They confronted him and forced him to re-
sign. He stepped down, appointing Ernest Shonekan, a civilian businessman, to run the government and organize new elections, but
Shonekan did not get the chance. He was easy prey for the ambitious defense chief General Sani Abacha, who, within four months, shouldered
him aside and took power himself in Nigeria's sixth successful coup.

∾

A man in the shadows for much of his career, rarely seen without dark
glasses, General Sani Abacha was the antithesis of the charming Babangida in many ways. Uninterested in the state of the economy but
street-smart and cunning, Abacha was a man unwilling to waste a moment courting favors when he did not have to and was ruthless in an almost un-Nigerian way.

"For all their faults, there was something to be said for Obasanjo,
Buhari, Babangida. There was nothing good about Abacha," a Nigerian
friend told me one year. "He was an embarrassment to Nigeria." Some
thought this was because of his upbringing—an unhappy childhood as
an outsider of humble origins, born in the Sabon Gari, or Strangers' District, of the north's biggest city, Kano, which had embittered him at an
early age.

Whether or not this was true, Abacha's ways were certainly different from—and more extreme than—those of past military rulers. The
most brutal leader Nigeria had yet known, Abacha clamped down everywhere on opposition, seeking no friends, and instead barring political
parties, student groups, and trade unions. The theft of public funds was

stepped up, money directed straight from the public coffers into Abacha's family accounts across the world, with little left over for the normal largesse.

Affronted that Abiola still claimed to be the rightful president, Abacha jailed him. The arrest set off a months-long strike in the oil sector. It was the biggest strike Nigeria had seen since independence, but Abacha crushed it easily. He hit hard at opponents in the unions, the delta, and in the press with arrests and, where that didn't work, with killings.

To carry these killings out, Abacha set up a hit squad, the Strike Force, bigger and more deadly than any previously known in Nigeria, to target his critics. Run by his chief aide, Major Hamza al-Mustapha, it murdered Kudirat Abiola, the wife of the 1993 election winner, and made attempts on the lives of the newspaper publisher Alex Ibru and the politician Abraham Adesanya. Abacha also jailed opponents such as Olusegun Obasanjo and Obasanjo's former number two, Shehu Musa Yar'Adua, on grounds that they were plotting against him. Yar'Adua then died in prison after being administered an injection by an army doctor Abacha sent.

In 1995, the general ordered the hanging of the writer Ken Saro-Wiwa for leading protests against the oil industry's devastation of the Niger Delta, ignoring all pleas for clemency.

Determined to profit from running the country, even if it caused economic decline, he set a dual exchange rate, one for officials and another for the public, and earned millions from what his aides called "round-tripping"—buying dollars at the cheap official rate and selling them on the street at three times the price. He ran down the state-run fuel refineries, denying them the repairs they needed to operate, and set up front companies that brought in the fuel the state needed, paying himself well to do so. And he crippled the state-run electricity company, diverting funds it needed for essential repairs into his own pockets, and set up businesses selling generators to firms left short of power.

Then, in June 1998, Abacha died suddenly. According to officials speaking in public, he had died from natural causes, a heart attack striking him down at home in the presidential villa. Off the record, journalists and diplomats were briefed that Abacha had been cavorting in a guesthouse at night with prostitutes and had overloaded on Viagra, triggering his attack. It was a plausible story, but why leak it? It seemed a deliberate attempt by officials to smear the late man's reputation in the conservative north and undermine whatever support he might have still had.

Then, later that day, Abacha's deputy, Abdulsalami Abubakar, was named his successor. And, a few weeks later, he told a Nigerian newsmagazine another and more interesting tale: that Abacha had planned on the day he died to retire him and other senior soldiers and arrest more for plotting a coup against him. The arrests were to have been announced at dawn on the day he died, Abubakar said. Immediately, the rumor mill started. Abubakar or his allies had had Abacha murdered, people said.

A month after Abacha died, Moshood Abiola, the man he had imprisoned for winning an election, died of a heart attack during a meeting with U.S. officials seeking to secure his release. Was it a coincidence? Nobody knew, but, with that, the military, who had feared handing power to the man they had jailed, agreed to be gone. They organized elections and left power.

෴

Difficult choices now awaited the political parties taking over. Most of those who emerged as politicians were old hands who had failed before and were not going to change the system soon. Parties needed funds to fight elections, and with no grassroots support, and with backers unwilling to provide funds without an immediate payback, unethical deal making was still the key to the system. Violence, intimidation, and bribery were the tools of power.

After four decades of freedom, this was the legacy of the military, and of the British before them, who had set up the system of government and shaped the constitution at independence. Ironically, in taking power, the military had done worse than anyone before and had also ruined itself. So now, not even the army could come to the rescue if needed.

A sketch of Edward Burns, my great great cousin, aged 22 in 1883, before he set off to Nigeria and Congo. Photo in the author's possession.

Hugo Marshall, my grandfather, inspects a guard of honor before his inauguration as lieutenant-governor of Western Nigeria in 1952. Pomp and ceremony was part of the job he least liked. Photo from family archives.

Hugo Marshall talks to reporters after his inauguration in 1952. The press has a major role to play in holding Nigeria's leaders to account but has not always been as effective as it could because of poor readership. Photo from family archives.

My grandfather with the Olubadan, traditional ruler of the southwestern city of Ibadan. Relations between the British and Nigeria's traditional rulers were often good. Photo from family archives.

Watched over by Yoruba leader Obafemi Awolowo, my grandfather signs the Western Region Local Government Law in 1953, a key stage in transferring power to Nigerians. Photo from family archives.

My grandmother, Susan Marshall, and Yoruba leader Obafemi Awolowo, in February 1954. Relations were generally friendly between the British and the Nigerian politicians who would succeed them. Photo from family archives.

A reception held in honor of Emmanuel Ifeajuna, seated seventh from left and next to my grandfather in 1954. A government clerk, he had just won the high jump gold at the Commonwealth Games in Vancouver. Twelve years later, as a soldier, he would be a leader of the country's first coup and kill the prime minister, Abubakar Tafawa Balewa, who was a friend of my grandfather's. Photo from family archives.

(left) *For well-off Lagos residents, one of the better places to relax is Bar Beach in the upmarket Victoria Island district. Once used by the military for public executions, it is today crowded with bars and open air eating places. Photo: Nicola Peckett. 2002.*

(below) *Sawmill smoke rises over Makoko, a slum district of Lagos where hundreds of thousands of the city's poorest live in wooden homes built on stilts over fetid waters. The district is home to a troubled young man I met called Johnson Afolabi. Photo: Nicola Peckett. 2002.*

(below) *A warning daubed on the wall of a house in Ibadan. Fraud is so widespread in Nigeria that the number 419—the section of the criminal code dealing with it—is a well-known synonym for the crime of deception. Photo: Nicola Peckett. 2002.*

Soldiers under a tree in Odi in the Niger Delta. Hundreds of people died when the army attacked the town in November 1999 to "teach a lesson" to the region after an attack on police. Photo: Peter Cunliffe-Jones. 1999.

A bridge between island homes in Akassa in the Niger Delta. More than 50 years after oil was discovered in the region, the Delta is still one of the poorest places in the world. Photo: Peter Cunliffe-Jones. 2003.

The National Mosque in Abuja is one of the capital's main landmarks. About half the population of Nigeria is Muslim, and the other half is Christian. Traditional faiths also survive. Photo: Peter Cunliffe-Jones. 2000.

Ahmed Sani, who was elected governor of the northern state of Zamfara in 1999 on a promise to restore Islamic law to the state. When 11 other northern states followed suit, Christian-Muslim clashes erupted in many parts of the country. Photo: Peter Cunliffe-Jones. 2000.

Camels in a market near Kano in 2001. The pace of life in the north is slower and more laid back than in the south. Photo: Nicola Peckett. 2001.

A typical family compound in a village in northwest Nigeria in 2003. Though men of the north have ruled the country for most of the 50 years since independence, the people of the region have benefited little. Photo: Peter Cunliffe-Jones. 2003.

Horsemen race across a square outside the emir's palace in the northern city of Katsina during the traditional durbar festival in 2001. The durbar ceremony takes place in most northern towns every year, a reaffirmation of loyalty to the region's traditional rulers. Photo: Nicola Peckett. 2001.

Crowds mass on the square outside the emir's palace in the main northern city of Kano following the end of the traditional durbar. Photo: Nicola Peckett. 2001.

CHAPTER 8

What You Left Behind

W hen I arrived in Nigeria in 1998, I was reluctant to admit my grandfather's role, or what my great-great cousin had done in Africa before him. The events that had occurred since independence—the collapse into civil war and misrule—seemed to cast judgment on those who'd played a part in events in the past. And I was fearful of how Nigerians would react to my family story.

Sometimes the discussion was hard to avoid. A year or two after arriving, I visited Ibadan, the sprawling city 100 miles northeast of Lagos that my grandfather long called home. I went there to meet Lam Adesina, the new governor of Oyo State, the heart of the old Western Region. I was working on a story on the government then in power.

Greeted by an aide in the state governor's house, I climbed a set of stairs, passing framed photographs of past rulers, civilian and military, arranged neatly on the wall. At the top, I stopped. The aide turned. Was something wrong? I shook my head. Staring back at me as I did

---

so was the familiar face of my grandfather in a formal state portrait, looking out along the hall. "No, nothing wrong," I said. "Just out of breath. That's all."

Hugo Marshall was a good man and a well-intentioned one. He believed in what he was doing and, in the early years, few people spoke up strongly against this British view. But from the 1930s onward, African and Asian voices emerged to challenge colonial rule. And after World War II, the tide of world opinion turned decisively against the colonial powers. And, by the 1950s, the later years of my grandfather's service, colonial rule was judged by many around the world to be "something very near a crime," as one writer said.

Raised in 1970s England, I took the modern view. No nation, no people, no race has the right to rule another. The economic exploitation and misrule of countries such as the Congo and Nigeria by Europeans was clearly a great wrong.

To my surprise, though, when I arrived in Nigeria, I met few Nigerians who where bitter about those they called "our Colonial Masters"—a phrase that always made me wince.

"Colonization was a positive thing," the old delta leader Harold Dappe-Biriye told me, in the study of his Port Harcourt home. "It brought us enlightenment, civilization, and greater freedom and democracy than we had ever had. The English language and education united us. If the British had not intervened as they did, we would not have advanced as we have." Once they were in power, the British eradicated slavery, ended the Yoruba wars, and introduced Western education and medicine, he said.

Even the Yoruba leader Obafemi Awolowo found good things to say of colonial rule. "There are many things which we do not like about the British rule," he wrote in 1960 as independence loomed. "But, if the truth is told, there are also a good many things which we have gained by our pupilage."[2] Peace and life under a "liberal" regime were the two he first mentioned.

"Enough with colonial guilt," a Nigerian friend told me, laughing, when I asked him what he thought. "It was wrong, but get over it. When do we admit our situation is down to us? Everyone was colonized at some point: America, Africa, Asia. Look what others have done since." When finally I told more Nigerian friends my grandfather had negotiated independence with Awolowo and Azikiwe, they expressed neither shock nor anger, but delight at the connection.

"Ah—at last," said one friend, slapping me heartily on the back, after I'd admitted my secret over a beer on the waterfront one evening. "Now I know why you came to Nigeria. You're coming back to rule us again. But look around," he laughed, gesturing at the untidy appearance of the beachfront and the gangs of hoodlums hanging out nearby. "Are you sure you really want to?" And he roared with laughter.

∾

Of course, the role the colonial powers had played in shaping the Africa of today cannot so easily be dismissed. As I see it, my late cousin's generation had stolen African land—from Nigeria to the Congo and beyond. Burns's diaries are the clearest admission of this theft. To take land and power, they had imposed their rule on hundreds of emerging states— Yoruba kingdoms, a northern caliphate, and Igbo societies among them—that, had they been left alone to develop, would have done so in a way truer to their history and so more stable in the end.

Instead, what had followed across Africa was political upheaval, exploitation, and scant development. Across the continent, port cities were built and named as capitals of countries that should never have been. Roads were dug and rails laid, but not to build the economies of the colonies—for that, the roads would have to have been laid in different directions, heading inland. Instead, they were built to bring the resources of Africa to the shore and thence to Europe. Like the other African colonies, Nigeria's economy was built to meet the wants of foreign powers—not to secure the prosperity of Nigerians.

Meanwhile, political foundations were not laid. Keeping traditional rulers in place, but dependent on the foreign power, diminished them in the eyes of the people they had once ruled. In 1932, my grandfather was posted to Okitipupa, the small town east of Lagos where the Biafran forces would later be stopped. One of his regular tasks there was to oversee payments made to "loyal"chiefs. This did nothing for Nigeria. The traditional rulers were soon seen as mere proxies of the British. And the politicians elected as the new rulers when the British left were not credible figures to most Nigerian eyes.

As one of them, Yoruba leader Obafemi Awolowo recognized that the British had created new rules of power, with election to office, and new rulers, the political class. But they had failed to prepare the media, the courts, and above all the people to hold their these new rulers to account. "Our teeming millions are still far from being sufficiently enlightened," Awolowo wrote on the eve of independence in 1960. "A public opinion strong and healthy enough to discourage irresponsibility and rascality in public life still has to be developed. A sense of civic responsibility on the part of the generality of our people is still to be cultivated," he declared.[3]

Instead, as World War II ended, my grandfather's generation built the new nations—unsteady, unstable—on false foundations and then left them to collapse. The crisis in Nigeria at independence was the fight for power between the regions. It was a crisis of Britain's making. The constitution they agreed on failed the country and led to a bloody civil war. This was not the intent but it was what happened. And those who paid the price were the Nigerians themselves. These days, when a house falls apart months or years after it is handed over, the builder and the architect are blamed, not the new owners or tenants. The quick collapse of Nigeria into civil war and misrule was the fault of the British.

Was this also the reason for the state of Nigeria today?

CHAPTER 9

Two Hours from Singapore

few months after elections in 2003, I flew out of Africa for Hong Kong and a new assignment in Asia. My time in Nigeria was over, and I was seeking a new challenge. Running the AFP news coverage of a region going from Kabul to Southeast Asia and the Pacific was it. For a few weeks, I spent my time in Hong Kong, settling in, getting to know the people and the news in the region. Then, bored of desk work, I picked up the phone and called the office secretary. I wanted a trip around the region.

Three days later, I was seated at the bar of the Raffles Hotel in Singapore, nursing a drink. I had half an hour to kill before a taxi came to take me to the airport. "So where are you going now? Back to Hong Kong?" my neighbor at the counter asked me. Mike was an Australian businessman in his fifties who'd been offering me his views on Asia for quite some time. I told him where I was headed: Indonesia.

"Indonesia," he replied. He was not sure I'd find it easy there. People didn't, he said. It was wild. Too wild for me. "The place is trouble. It's two hours from Singapore. But it's another world."

When I flew in to Jakarta a few hours later, what I saw below me looked oddly familiar. Hong Kong and Singapore are smart, modern cities, wealthy and content. Jakarta looked different. The airport, surrounded by miles of low-rise red-roofed buildings and green vegetation, could have been Lagos, I thought. I studied the guidebook I'd brought with me. Indonesia, it said, is a sprawling archipelago lying between Malaysia and Australia, home to more than 240 million people. Jakarta is its Lagos, a vast, sprawling port city teeming with a population of 15 million. Chaotic and noisy, it said.

Emerging from the airport, I was hit immediately by the blanket of warm, wet air common to the tropics worldwide. Then my taxi took me off on the long drive into the city center. I wound down the window and breathed in a familiar mix of car fumes and wood smoke, rising from shacks by the roadside. When we stopped at an intersection, crowds of noisy children emerged as they would elsewhere to hawk their wares, offering us everything from spicy foods to soft drinks, typewriter covers to newspapers. Setting off again, we passed fishing villages and drove past flooded rice paddies and on into the city.

Half an hour later, after dropping my bags at the hotel, I crossed the road and went up to meet the staff. I was met at the elevator by the Jakarta bureau chief, Alain, and went in with him. Viktor Tjahjadi, one of the local reporters, turned and waved a greeting. "Welcome to Indonesia," he said. "Welcome to the land of the politically confused." After three months confined to the smart business districts of Hong Kong, and two days in Singapore, I felt I'd finally come home.

ॐ

Separated by many miles of land and ocean, Indonesia and Nigeria seem to me to be twins parted at birth. Both are the giants of their region, overflowing with people. Indonesia is the world's fourth-largest nation and Nigeria the eighth. Indonesia's people speak more than 200 languages and follow three or four major religions. Nigeria's speak more than 400 languages and follow two world religions and indigenous beliefs. Even the cultures seem similar in many ways: the shadow-puppet theater of Java and the masked Yoruba masquerades, the use of batik and of tie-dye, the writers telling tales of colonial conquest and cultural loss.

Politically and historically, the countries compare well. Both are recent creations, ancient states formed and then governed as one country by Europeans around the start of the last century. Both countries were subject to indirect rule. Both countries are home to large immigrant communities—the Chinese in Indonesia and the Lebanese in Nigeria—important members of the business class. Since World War II and independence, both countries have suffered turbulent histories. Their first coups were launched within months of each other—in September 1965 in Indonesia and in January 1966 in Nigeria. And their dictators left power within months of each other too, in May 1998 in Jakarta and in May 1999 in Abuja.

In Indonesia, the coup that brought a dictator to power began with a small group of junior air force officers, drawn from a group loyal to the leftist president, striking the army that threatened his rule. Six generals died, but the soldiers missed several key targets, and, within hours, the rightists struck back. Over the following year, the Right launched a wave of terror against those it blamed for the killings—the suspected communists—and sidelined the weakened president. The slaughter left more than half a million dead.

By the middle of the next year, the rightists had consolidated their hold. In 1967, they appointed their leader, General Suharto, as head of state. And for 31 years he ruled uninterrupted. During that time, Indonesia, like Nigeria, would struggle with the impact of oil, secessionist movements, and civil unrest. Its leaders would gain notoriety for corruption, jailing opponents, and suppressing human rights.

Driving around the city on my way to meetings with newspaper editors and clients, I'd see the same things I saw in Nigeria. There were districts for the rich and districts for the poor, all cheek by jowl. Passing the tall wrought-iron gates of the rich, I'd see the same colonnaded mansions with fancy lawns and drives that I saw in Nigeria. And around the corner, the same shacks and squalor.

Indonesia was the Asian Nigeria, I told myself. It had the same sort of people, the same feel. It too had found oil at independence, and it had the same colonial history and the same recent past. It was no wonder that I felt so at home.

෴

But Indonesia is not Nigeria. Talking to the editor of an Indonesian newsmagazine the next day, I was struck by a statistic he mentioned in passing. In Indonesia, he said, the life expectancy of a child at birth had risen since independence from 45 to 70 years. In Nigeria, I thought, life expectancy remained stuck at 45 years. It was a startling difference.

I checked that figure and some others. In Indonesia, when Suharto took power, six in ten people lived in poverty, a similar story to Nigeria at the time. Three decades later, the Indonesian figure was under two in ten. In Nigeria it was up to seven. Per capita income in Indonesia had risen more than sixfold since the mid-1960s, unlike in Nigeria, where it had dropped. Basic health care was now strikingly better in Indonesia than in Nigeria, and the same was true for education. People in Indonesia were even eating better. They had a higher daily calorie intake. In Nigeria, it had fallen.

At independence, Indonesia performed as well as Nigeria on most measures and worse on some. But now it was doing better on almost all fronts: growth, average income, health, education, clean water, and electricity. Indonesia was still clearly a troubled country. It had suffered political and economic upheaval and still suffered Islamic militancy and unrest. But even this was changing. It was holding elections that the world applauded and emerging from its troubles, while Nigeria was getting nowhere.

The parallels, of course, are not exact, I told a friend. The two countries lie 7,000 miles apart, on different continents. With different neighbors, the two countries are, of course, subject to the effect of surrounding countries that can pull a country up or push it down. But they have more in common than most. They are both big, complex nations, recently formed, with a similar colonial history, blessed or cursed by oil, and weakened by corruption, dictatorship, unrest, and misrule.

If the colonial history was about the same, I needed to understand why they'd developed differently. I set my sights for Nigeria again. I would start out with oil.

CHAPTER 10

The Cost of Oil

T**he** *cost of oil*—discovered in Nigeria in 1956—can be measured in a person's blood. Mine became infected with a mosquito's bite. The first thing I knew of it was three days later, with an ache in the back of my head, so faint I barely noticed it at first. I was on a plane to Paris, heading for a meeting. It was 1999. The ache started out in my neck at the place where the spine goes into the base of the brain. An hour later, it began to spread, darts of pain shooting through my temples and behind my eyes, making me wince. I thought at first it was sunstroke. I'd played tennis with a friend the previous afternoon and was sure that was the reason. But I've had that before, and this was much worse. One minute I was hot. The next I was cold and shivering. Looking around me on the plane, filled with businessmen heading for Europe, I could tell that nobody else seemed to have noticed a sudden drop in temperature. I did. Minutes later, I started to sweat.

We landed in Paris. The airport, the train journey, and the taxi ride went by in a blur: wet city streets and early morning light. I had not booked myself into a hotel. I was going to house-sit for vacationing friends. Their apartment was a beautiful, book-lined affair just off the Rue Richelieu, close to AFP headquarters on the Place de la Bourse. Sleep, I decided. I needed sleep. But first, on a cool day, I needed to change my shirt. I'd sweated so much I had to wring it out in the sink.

I woke up on the couch a few hours later. I ached as though my bones had shrunk. I was cold. I showered to get warm. Suddenly, my stomach leapt and I dived to the sink to be sick. Then I started sweating again. I staggered to the meeting that had brought me to Paris in the first place. When I got there, a colleague took one look at me and then put me in a car and drove me to the Hôpital Bichat in the northern suburbs. Twenty minutes later, after draining me of a little blood, the nurse was back. It was cerebral malaria, she said. I must have caught it a few days earlier in the Niger Delta. Later, I would look up its effects. The symptoms are fever and chills, aches, and nausea. Untreated, it causes coma and death. She prescribed a course of strong drugs and several days' rest in bed.

Without that cheap treatment, I would have died. My blood was soon fine.

∾

A few months later, I was back in the delta for a feature I was writing on gangs, politics, and poverty. I took a boat out into the swamps with a Nigerian colleague. John knew the delta well and said he'd take me to a village he'd been to before. It was a hot day, the white light of the sun bouncing off the surface of the water as we left. Our first stop was a row of houses by a riverbank. The river was slow-moving. As we went ashore, flies rose from shallow pools of brown water gathered between the roots of the overhanging mangrove trees. We climbed the bank. Next to the houses, overripe fruit—mango and papaya—rotted on a garbage pile. A couple of scrawny chickens scratched nearby.

As we approached the row of houses, a woman called Are Ekate emerged from the house nearest to the river. It was a simple cinder block construction with a corrugated iron roof. The door was open. In the windows at the front and on one side there was no glass, just a scrap of heavy red cloth hanging lankly in the heat. There were two beds: one for the mother and three of her four children, the other a makeshift affair of sticks and a blanket for her ailing fourth child—Judith.

Judith was two. She had malaria: bad blood. She was sweating. As I looked, I saw a droplet of sweat trickle down her neck to stop in the dark hollow of her throat. Her eyes were glazed, her head moving listlessly from side to side. She had just been sick. Her breathing was fast and shallow, and the yellow-brown bones of her tiny chest rose and fell with each rapid breath. The mother, a market trader, had already lost one child to malaria, she told us, and was desperate not to lose another.

"Give her something," she said, grabbing at my hand. She had called us in thinking perhaps we could help. But what could we do? We were not doctors. Are's demands were insistent nonetheless. "Give her something to make her better."

We knelt down and felt Judith's pulse. It was racing. "It's too fast. She's dying," John whispered. I felt we should do something but didn't know what. I wetted a cloth with some bottled water I'd brought and put it on the child's forehead, the bottle to her lips. I had a box of aspirin but nothing for a child with malaria. "It's too late to do anything," John whispered in my ear.

Are held my hand and asked me not to leave. Her daughter was dying, and I could not stop it happening. So I did the only thing I could think of. As Are murmured to her child, I sat there with her and my colleague in silence as Judith died.

Finally, minutes later, the breathing stopped. Are went silent too. She did not cry out. We sat in the dark. I mumbled condolences, gripped her hand again, apologized we could do no more, and walked outside with John.

There are things that can be done to stop malaria; simple things. I knew this much, but not how to say it; not then. It was important for her three other children that Are clear away still water from around the house. It was important to move the village trash pile further away too. Above all, it was important to get mosquito nets for the children, to be let down over their beds at night. And she should get drugs that worked for a child too.

This was "oil-rich" Nigeria, I said to myself. I'd hoped that, if a child was ill, they'd have a doctor and a clinic. But, of course, I was wrong.

As we left, I asked John why so many people succumbed to malaria in the Niger Delta, where thousands die of it every year. "They are poor," he said. "It is oil. They cannot fish and farm as before. Most people don't have bed-nets. Often, if bed-nets are given out, they are not used. People don't want to spoil them by using them too often. And they can't afford the drugs. Or, if they can, they stop the treatment part way through to save some for next time. They get bad blood."

"It's not their fault," he added. "It's poverty. It's oil. It's the government. It's why there is no health care here at all."

ↄ

The boat took us back to Yenagoa, the capital of Bayelsa State, a town flush with oil money. We swung in and out through the creeks, passing villages perched on the riverbanks, ducking ugly oil pipelines, and overtaking dugout canoes paddled by a lone man or woman sitting at the back. The boats we passed were laden with supplies from chickens and plantain to motorbike parts and crates of drink. "Everything they need in the delta has to be carried in by boat so it costs twice what it does ashore," John said.

As we rounded a sandbank, I saw the low-rise buildings of Yenagoa come into view. It had taken us half an hour on the way down. Against the current, it had taken us an hour to get back.

"The governor's in," John said. I looked across and there, indeed, was the governor's yacht, large and sleek. Too large, John said, to get through the narrow waterways that make up much of the state. How many bednets would that have paid for? I wondered to myself. How much does Bayelsa State spend on health care and how much on the governor and his luxuries?

～

Since the civil war ended, Nigeria has earned more than $400 billion from oil, and yet both the number and the percentage of people living in poverty have gone up in that time: up from 35 percent to 70 percent of a growing population. In the boom years of the 1970s, when the world price of oil soared, the government spent money like water, but, while some was well spent, most was mismanaged. Projects were started but not completed or, if completed, were not maintained. Money was misappropriated and stolen. The nonoil economy was starved of the attention it needed. A few became richer. Most became poorer.

Before it found oil, Nigeria was an agricultural producer. Farming and manufacturing gave people work. But when oil prices leapt in the 1970s, and with no incentive to stay on the land, people flocked to take their chance in the cities. In just three short years, the amount of land used for farming shrank by 60 percent as people headed to the cities for jobs that were not there to be found. And, today, oil dominates a shrunken economy. It accounts for 95 percent of all the country's export earnings. It brings in money, but the money is not spread around.

So oil is a problem. But it's not the oil itself. It is the way it is used. It is the effect it's allowed to have. Other countries have oil. Indonesia has oil. It hasn't been ruined by oil. But the way that oil is produced and the way it is used have ruined Nigeria.

&

First, there is the way it is produced. Elsewhere in the world—in the United States or Europe and even Asia—the pipes are buried underground to minimize disruption to local people. In the delta they run aboveground, close to people's homes and fields, dripping fuel and polluting land and water. The poor can't fish and farm to feed their families. In 2008, a Nigerian environmental agency reported 1,150 major oil-spill sites across the delta abandoned by oil companies, all leaking into the water people drink and the land they live off.[1] Tests last decade found hydrocarbons in drinking water at levels more than 360 times what is permitted in Europe.[2] Crops, if they can grow, are tainted with chemicals. The catches are smaller, in part because of overfishing, in part because of pollution. Unable to earn a living from farming and fishing, the inhabitants of the region have become dependent on the state or oil firms for work.

But oil and gas do not create many jobs. It takes just a few men and machines to run an oil rig or pumping station—hundreds, not thousands. The pipes suck oil up out of the ground, and the firms put money in the hands of the owners and the government. But unless you're either of those, this is of little help to you. With oil and gas, there are few jobs created for the skilled farmer or fisherman. There is even no need for roads and bridges, only for pipes and pumping stations, of little use to people in getting to work or going to school.

And oil money draws the wrong men into power, men like Diepreye Alamieyeseigha, the owner of the yacht I'd just seen, men who misuse the money oil brings. Corruption means that the money earned by the state does not go to education, health care, roads, or bridges. Hundreds of billions of dollars have been squandered or stolen since 1970, campaigners say. The problem here is how the leaders behave.

∽

In 2000, a year after army rule ended, I went to meet Governor Alamieyeseigha. He is a slow-moving man, with a wide smile and heavy-lidded eyes. I met him at his office. Asked to pass through airport-style security, I was taken upstairs and welcomed into a spacious room with a ring of leather chairs around the walls and a huge table and armchairs in the center.

Every election in Nigeria is a battle for control of oil money. The election in 1999 was no exception and, in the delta, it was nothing like a fair vote at all. With the oil industry based in the region, the delta states get a higher share of the national oil revenue than other regions, and the governors can control these funds. They can also make deals with oil firms and others on the side. And, put together, this makes delta politics a deadly game and an electoral farce.

On election day, February 1999, a gang hired by Alamieyeseigha roamed the swamps by boat, fighting off the thugs hired by his rivals and intimidating voters into staying at home. Once in control of the creeks, they stole the ballot papers delivered by boat, then stuffed ballot boxes, inflated voter returns, and bribed or pressured election officials into fixing the results. It was a contest in rigging, not a battle for the voters' minds. In many places, no one showed up at the polling stations, which stayed closed all day.

A year on, and, sitting back in his armchair, the man who had "won" the contest talked about the delta and the problems of the region. Abuja, the capital, was not doing what it should for the delta, he complained. I then turned the conversation to him and asked how he was doing himself. "You are governor of one of the poorest places in

Nigeria, the poorest state in the Niger Delta," I told him. "But you seem to live very well."

"In Nigeria," he told me, with a wolfish smile, "people do not want their governor to be a pauper. It would not look right. I do all right for myself. I do all right for the people of Bayelsa."

He was, of course, half right. Three years later, police in London would make clear how well Alamieyeseigha had done for himself. Not content with his sumptuous yacht, paid for from public funds, and $25 million spent on his official mansion, he had acquired four London properties and a penthouse in Cape Town. He had opened bank accounts for himself, his wife, and his children, and had acquired properties elsewhere. When the police called, the cash equivalent of £915,000 in pounds, dollars, and euros lay scattered around the master bedroom of his flat in West London, some lying loose on the floor, some stuffed into the pockets of a dressing gown. And, acting on information from Nigeria, they charged him with money laundering.[3]

Such profligacy and theft were not the only reasons that Alamieyeseigha was a disaster for Bayelsa. In fact, it was his meanness with money that caused the first real crisis.

After the election in 1999, the gang he'd used to help get him elected felt he was slow in coming up with the payments he'd promised. Out of pocket, the gang started freelancing, carrying out robberies and carjackings on the side until, in October that year, the police sent in a team to arrest them.

The first time they did so, the police went lightly armed. A shot was fired, and mayhem followed. Seven policemen and three gang members were killed. The rest of the gang escaped. The next day, the police returned, more heavily armed, but this time the gang knew what was coming. In the shootout that followed, five more policemen and two gang members were killed but the rest of the gang got away. This was too much. If a gang could do this and get away with it, others might get the same idea. So the following week, just six months after civilian rule was restored, commanders ordered soldiers out of their barracks in nearby Port Harcourt to proceed west, to the town where the gang was last reported: the town of Odi, a few miles from Yenagoa.

Setting off from Port Harcourt at dawn, the soldiers soon reached the outskirts of the town. After a brief exchange of gunfire, the gang fled. That did not stop the soldiers. They could deal with the gang later. Their orders were to send a wider message to the region and, to do it, they had brought with them a battery of mortars. At noon, they started hitting the town where hundreds more, too old or ill to flee, were still trapped. For two hours, the pounding went on. When finally it stopped, most of those in the town had died, and most homes were in ruins.[4]

Having just returned to Lagos from a trip abroad, I reached Odi two days later. The soldiers were still ringing the town and patrolling the streets. I negotiated a pass at the main checkpoint and drove in. Some buildings were still smoldering. They'd been looted, then set ablaze. By the roadside, or underneath rubble, I could see a few bodies still lying around and body parts where the mortars had scored a direct hit. Almost all the houses were in ruins, the walls blackened and crumbling, the roofs open to the sky. A few dazed people were wandering around.

Walking cautiously up the main street, I spotted a group of elderly residents who'd returned that morning. They looked shell-shocked. About ten in all, they had gathered under a tree. Fifty yards away, a party of soldiers lolled in the shade. I spoke to one of the residents, Anthony Ogbise, 80 years old, a retired teacher, now homeless.

I asked him what had happened. "The soldiers came outside the town," he said quietly, his voice a whisper, eyes darting to the men in uniform nearby. "They fired on us and came in. They killed who they wanted."

Did he know why they'd come? I asked. "They said there was a gang here but they had fled. So the soldiers took our things and burned our homes. My house, my clothes, my Bible are all gone," he said.

A policeman came over to find out what I was doing and asked me to leave. I showed him my papers. I had army permission to enter the town. It did not matter. I had outstayed my welcome. Driving out of town a few minutes later, I stopped the car. An odor of flesh, of corpses rotting in the heat, was coming from nearby bushes. Judging from the stench, it was clear that a large number of bodies were lying there. I got out and took a step toward the side of the road. As I did so, a soldier appeared from the bushes, leveled his gun at me, and ordered me away.

I drove to Port Harcourt to meet the men in charge of the operation. "The people in Odi had tolerated these criminals, these attacks on security forces," the army spokesman, Captain John Agim, told me at headquarters. He was not embarrassed by what the soldiers had done: shooting, shelling, looting, and burning. "It was a show of force. The intention was to let them know they cannot continue like that. That has been achieved. The message to the delta is clear. The delta has been taught a lesson."

But what was the lesson? Oil money draws malefactors into power, men such as Alamieyeseigha. To get the money that comes from being a governor in the delta, he had hired a gang to rig his "election." Once he had won power, Alamieyeseigha cut the gang loose. "They are nothing to do with me anymore," he had told me when I visited. "I did not order the attack on the town." Now, he had got his yacht and, as I would discover later, a vast stash of wealth in cash, in the bank, and in homes in London and elsewhere. He had not built schools for the poor or created jobs. He had not built clinics in the villages to help people like Are and Judith Ekate. He had cheated the gang who had got him into power. And now hundreds of people from Odi were dead or without a home.

Four years after that first election, I went back to Bayelsa and back to Odi. It was 2003. New polls were being held across the country, and, as before, the worst violence and vote-rigging came in the delta. In Odi, the voter list presented by officials was a joke. Though hundreds of people had died in the attack on the town in 1999, the voter list was unchanged from the one used then. When officials announced the results, they said that 100 percent of those registered, then and now, had voted and that every last one had voted for the ruling party.

"Election? What election?" asked Koko Manana, a community leader, when I called around the next day to ask about the voting in Odi. "There was no election here. There was no voting. Dead men voted if anyone did at all."

Later that day, the governor was returned to power.

And what would he do for the next little girl like Judith Ekate? Nothing.

ॐ

The corruption of politics by oil is not restricted to the delta. It has spread throughout Nigeria, affecting politics in every town and at every level. Africa's most populous nation is a big country. But the impact on politics of oil, drawn from the delta's swamps, extends right across the nation. Oil money is what politicians across Nigeria fight for. It washes around in Abuja, the capital. It floods through the 36 states of north and south. And it seeps down into the level Nigerians consider the most corrupt of all: the 774 local governments spread right across the nation.

"Look at that house," Mr. Lakanu, my Lagos neighbor, told me one day as we walked together along the dusty road we both called home. He was pointing to a brand-new residence going up behind high walls on our road. "That man has never done anything, never built anything. He is just an Area Boy," a member of the gangs who control the Lagos streets, my neighbor said. "What has he done? He has not contributed to our society. He has not built a business. His gangs just stole the local election here. He used to live in a shack. Now, all of a sudden, he is council chairman, and he's a wealthy man."

Oil money, coming from the delta, was drawing gang leaders into local as well as national politics in Lagos and around the country, putting them in charge of budgets and shaping local affairs.

It was 2003, and a national election was looming. A few days later, I flew north to a fly-blown village in northwest Nigeria, a few miles from the northern border. I was there to see the village chief. I wanted to know how people in the north would vote, how he would ask his village to vote, and how the system was affected by oil money.

Entering the chief's house, I learned that the teams of the two main candidates for state governor had visited a few days apart and offered him money to swing the village vote their way. He'd accepted the money from both. He would not say how much they had paid nor who had paid most. But he admitted that his vote—and his control of his villagers' vote with it—was up for sale.

Where had the money come from to do this? Neither candidate had a business big enough to fund this sort of campaigning, so far as I knew. And the parties they ran for had few supporters paying fees to finance such an operation. Trace it back, I suspect, and the money would have come from oil. Governors, local councilors, state senators, and senators: oil money had gotten to them all.

ຕ

Countries that do control their oil—the way it is produced and where the money goes—benefit from it. From Aberdeen, Scotland, to Houston, Texas, oil is seen as a blessing, not a curse. It provides a few jobs and much revenue that funds government programs and investments in other sectors. In Indonesia it was the same.

Where production and the flow of money are not controlled, they pollute the country's environment and its politics. "Producing oil seems to be a bit like taking cocaine," said the journalist Nicholas Shaxson. "If you are healthy it might invigorate you." If you are not, "it can do you serious harm."[5] The question to me was why some countries would be vulnerable and others not; why oil would benefit a country such as Indonesia but would do so much harm in a country such as Nigeria.

Despite the countries' outward similarities, Indonesia seems to have escaped the oil curse. Born in the days of colonial rule, Indonesia's oil industry grew rapidly after independence, to produce 2 million barrels per day. But unlike in Nigeria, oil did not squeeze out the other sectors of the economy. Instead, with government investment funded by its oil receipts, other sectors grew stronger and the share of export earnings provided by oil and gas shrank, from three-quarters in the 1970s to under one-fifth today.

How did this happen? I asked Bambang Harymurti, an Indonesian journalist. "Struggle is the reason," he said. The Indonesian army and politicians had stolen much of the country's oil. Suharto, who ruled for three decades, was very corrupt. But, dictator though he was, Suharto felt pressure throughout his long rule from the media, the business elite, the urban poor, and the countryside to perform, Bambang said.

Indonesia is a place where popular revolts have happened several times in the past. So, while lining his own pockets and those of his family and friends, Suharto made sure he diversified the economy away from dependence on oil. He developed sectors, such as fishing, farming, and tourism, that he knew would absorb labor, cut poverty, and reduce the risk of a popular uprising against him. "The pressure on Suharto to perform or be ousted was the key," Bambang said.

～

Nigeria's own rulers have, of course, been challenged to perform—in the delta and elsewhere. Since independence, Nigerian governments have known to talk up development plans for both the delta and Nigeria. In 1961, a year after independence, the new government established an agency, the Niger Delta Development Board, to develop the region. Almost every decade since has produced another organization, adding another dollop to the country's alphabet soup of bodies tasked with development. The latest is the Niger Delta Development Commission (NDDC).

But, though the money pledged for each one was always impressive—and the amounts grew over the years—the performance never was. Around the delta, and around the country, hundreds of projects were declared under way. Holes would be dug and foundations laid. The next day, grainy photos would appear in the papers showing a politician standing beside a digger or earthmover, inspecting the project site. But, in the months that followed, no road, bridge, school, or clinic would rise up after they'd left. Often, all there would be was a hole in the ground. In 1999, a survey found more than 800 such abandoned projects littering the delta landscape alone. The money pledged to the projects had disappeared.

In most parts of the country, people seemed to accept this as how things were and would always be. But, in the delta things were seen differently. This was not simply "government money," sprouting from the ground, for politicians to do with as they wished—which was how many Nigerians saw it. In the delta, government money was seen as oil money, coming from the delta at great cost to the delta people. And, by 1990, some delta people had had enough.

Born in 1941 at Bori in Rivers State, in the eastern delta, Ken Saro-Wiwa is perhaps the region's most famous son. As a young man he found a certain fame and fortune with his writings. For a few years, he entered politics, working as education commissioner under a military regime. But he was soon dismissed after calling for fairer treatment for the delta people. In the 1980s, he found new success as writer and producer of one of the country's most popular TV soaps, *Basi & Co.* And, in 1990, he put this popularity to use to campaign for his delta people.

The issue that formed the focus of his campaign was the plight of his Ogoni homeland. With a population estimated at half a million, the Ogoni made up just one-twentieth of the delta's then 10 million people. They lived in an area of only 400 square miles. But, thanks to Saro-Wiwa's campaigning, for a few years in the 1990s the Ogonis grabbed the world's attention. They brought to the world's notice the damaging impact of oil operations on all the people of the Niger Delta.

To all who would listen, Saro-Wiwa explained that Ogoniland's problems started in 1958, when the forerunners of the Anglo–Dutch oil group Royal Dutch/Shell began operations in the region. This was two years after its first oil strike elsewhere in the delta. Over three decades, the company would dig 96 wells in Ogoni territory, bringing nine fields onstream and producing, at its height, 28,000 barrels of crude per day. But, with the pipelines running close to people's homes and through their fields, pollution ruined the land while flares from the gas towers fouled the air, making it hard for some to breathe, causing acid rain, and keeping people awake at night.

For years, the Ogoni called for change and waited to see some good come to the community in return for oil taken. But most of the few jobs created went not to them but to other Nigerians, better connected to those in power. So, in 1990, Saro-Wiwa and a group of Ogoni chiefs and elders got together and announced the creation of the Movement for the Survival of the Ogoni People (MOSOP), a nonviolent group set up to push for change. It published an Ogoni bill of rights listing their grievances and demands. Among them, it called for protection of the environment, for greater autonomy, and for a larger share of the oil revenue to return to the region.

Articulate and well-connected in the media, Saro-Wiwa and MOSOP would prove an embarrassment to the military government and the oil firms, Shell in particular. At first, the campaign was relatively low-level. Then, on January 4, 1993, MOSOP staged a protest attracting 300,000 people, more than half the Ogoni population. International attention grew, and so did that of the military.

For the army and for Shell, the Ogoni Day rally held on January 4, 1993, made MOSOP a major problem. The group was drawing attention to things they wanted no one to know—not just in Ogoniland but also across the delta. Saro-Wiwa was detained, and MOSOP members were beaten and jailed. Then, in May 1994, the military found a way to break the organization. On May 21, four elderly Ogoni chiefs opposed to the MOSOP campaign were brutally murdered. Saro-Wiwa was not present, but the military accused him of incitement and charged him and eight supporters with the murder. Claiming that law and order had broken down, it then sent in a military task force, headed by a notorious commander, Major Paul Okuntimo, to "restore peace." And he launched a wave of repression, with killings and beatings such as the Ogoni had never before seen.

The trial of Saro-Wiwa and his eight supporters took place the following year before a special military tribunal. As soon as it opened, it was clear that the tribunal did not plan on giving the defendants a fair hearing. As the prosecution started its case, the defense lawyers resigned en masse in protest at the handling of the case. Their protests—and those of international experts—were ignored. When the hearing ended, the judges found all the men guilty. General Abacha, who as a junior officer in Rivers State had known Saro-Wiwa well, ignored pleas for clemency from world leaders, including the South African president Nelson Mandela. And, on November 10, 1995, Saro-Wiwa and his supporters were hanged, their bodies then thrown into a lime pit to destroy their remains.

After the executions, MOSOP broke apart and split into rival factions. It faded as a protest organization. But the outcry over the killing of Saro-Wiwa had spurred the oil companies into action. They had suffered bad publicity and now had to do something. Oil firms announced their own development projects, unable to rely on the government to drive progress. Shell, Chevron, and the other firms built schoolrooms, clinics, and roads in areas where they operated. They gave out money to local communities and created jobs. They pledged protection for the environment.

It was good, but it was not enough to make a difference. Development was neither the firms' real interest nor their area of expertise. Clinics were built but, with no one to equip or run them, they served little purpose and were soon abandoned. Schools were set up but, without teachers, they went to waste. Worse, by favoring one village over another with their projects, the oil firms created new tensions between the communities. While the military stayed in power, the tensions were largely suppressed. When they left, fighting flared.

Soon everyone in the delta was a rebel. Some of the new groups were Ijaw nationalists, fighting for the interests of their Ijaw people against the other peoples of the delta. Others appeared to be led by people seeking only money for themselves, people with close links to politicians, the army, and even the oil firms they claimed to be fighting against. When I went down to the delta in 1998, I met many such men.

In 2006, a new group formed called the Movement for the Emancipation of the Niger Delta (MEND). Seemingly more serious and better armed than previous outfits, its attacks grew in number and audacity over the months that followed. Over the next four years, people claiming to be MEND fighters blew up oil pipelines and snatched oil workers from rigs and drilling platforms. MEND's spokesmen claimed that the attacks were justified pressure on the oil industry and said the ransom payments were used to fund community-support programs and to buy more weapons. In 2009, MEND staged fresh attacks on pipelines and platforms miles out to sea and as far away as Lagos. It made things difficult for the oil firms. Companies started to leave the delta or to scale back operations. Oil production suffered. State revenue started to fall.

MEND was not the only operation. Alongside it, purely criminal gangs, the military, and politicians cooperated in drawing oil off from pipelines, loading it up into ships, and selling it overseas—"bunkering" it was called—stealing from the oil firms and the authorities. And it became big business, worth hundreds of millions of dollars every year.

In an attempt to turn the tide, the government in August 2009 announced an amnesty for MEND fighters who turned in their weapons and sought new government jobs. The next month, it declared the exercise a success with the surrender of thousands of guns by former rebels. In October that year, it announced plans to pay 10 percent of government oil revenues directly to the delta communities in the future. In response, MEND declared a temporary truce. A real stake for the communities in the oil business would ensure peace and development in the delta, a government spokesman told me in Abuja. Was pressure from the delta people finally working?

Few were convinced the plan would succeed. Most people thought the money that was pledged would be "diverted" long before it reached the people. Promised jobs would not be found. To bring peace, the government would not only need to get jobs and money to the people, but it would also need to stop the trade in stolen oil, which many thought was a big factor in causing the unrest. At present, there is too much money to be made by groups stealing oil for them to lay down their weapons, a friend working in the region told me when the new policy was announced. By January 2010, after waiting for signs of real change, MEND was frustrated with the lack of progress. It called off its self-declared truce. Dissatisfied ex-militants left the training camps they had been brought to, awaiting training that never came. In March, militants exploded two car bombs in Warri as officials gathered to discuss how the amnesty was working.

To really change, the delta indeed needs more than an amnesty and a few extra dollars. It needs a change of heart at the top. It needs a big investment in roads and bridges. It needs a cleanup of its land and water to allow people to farm and fish. It needs investment in small industry to create new jobs. And that was still a long way from happening.

$$\infty$$

Still, the rebellion had shown Nigeria what was needed to get that change of heart—what it has needed since its earliest days, through the years of exploitation under the early kingdoms, colonial rule, the military regimes, and today. Nigeria needs its people to put pressure on those in power to use the money well, and to govern well, if it is to develop as Indonesia and other countries have. It needs pressure on those in power to build roads and railways, invest in farming and manufacturing, and provide services such as health and education.

It can happen. I had seen pressure work before at a local level, in 2003, at Akassa, a small island at the southernmost tip of the delta, the place where George Goldie set up his first company headquarters and close to the spot that Edward Burns visited in 1883. Akassa today is not the headquarters of anything. Long since abandoned by trading companies, it is just an island jutting out into the sea at the furthest reaches of the Niger River. But it's an interesting place to see what can happen, even in an oil region, if pressure is applied on leaders.

I went to visit a friend working in Akassa on a community project. Phil Arkell was a social worker from England whom I'd known in Lagos. He'd worked then on a scheme providing vocational training to the disabled in the city. Now he was heading a project to get a whole community working.

Partly funded by donations from a Norwegian oil company and partly from a Paris-based NGO, the project Phil was running did not, like most delta projects, aim to build new buildings but to develop community capacity. It aimed to help the community help itself.

In Kongho, the main town in Akassa, the whole community was involved in what they were doing. Women ran a nursery school and literacy group. A community bank gave out microloans to small businesses. But besides the help from the project leaders, the community got precious little help from elsewhere. Despite the flood of oil money drawn out of the delta every day, those living there in a community such as Akassa got next to nothing in return from the oil companies or the government.

And, weeks before I arrived, Akassa decided to challenge the status quo. Spurred on by their youth leaders, a group of elders took to the radio to denounce the local council chairman for siphoning off money meant for Kongho. "It was amazing the effect it had. He protested of course. But he had been humbled on air," Lucy Oweigha, the chair of one of the project's leading bodies, the Akassa Women's Association, told me gleefully when I arrived a few weeks later. Within days, the local government had started work on a new jetty that Kongho had been asking for for years. And it promised work on a string of other projects, she said.

The list of what Akassa still needed was long. The community needed bridges as well as boats. It needed a better clinic and traveling doctor services. It needed good schools. It needed jobs for the young and old. With the exception of bridges and boats, the list was much the same across most of Nigeria.

"The trick is to keep up the pressure, when you see that pressure works," Lucy told me. "Now the lesson needs to spread outside the delta."

"It's not oil," she said.

CHAPTER 11

Corruption and Trust

"I *t's corruption,*" said my friend Yemi, the clapped-out engine of his aging blue Mercedes straining as we drove up the hill. "Corruption has been a problem in Nigeria since the first days of independence, long before oil money started to flow." Whether Nigeria has oil or not, it makes no difference, he said. "It would still have corruption."

Sitting on the dashboard was a well-thumbed copy of *A Man of the People,* Chinua Achebe's fourth novel, written in 1966, long before oil money became the main interest of the country's politicians. I'd been reading it while staying at the small guesthouse Yemi ran in Port Harcourt. Corruption was a major theme, even then.

Yemi had agreed that morning to drive me to the capital, Abuja. And, as so often, our conversation had turned to the troubles of Nigeria. I'd been trying to push my argument about oil—an economist friend's theory that Nigeria needs the price of oil to collapse to wean its politicians off the money oil provided and force them to build a real

---

economy instead. To Yemi, it was fine as a theory but was missing the point. "The price of oil makes no difference," he said. "If oil was for free our politicians would steal the air we breathe and charge us for it. With a people like ours, it is corruption that matters," he said.

"You see!" he exclaimed. As we were talking, we'd reached the top of the rise and, up ahead, saw a couple of soldiers standing in the middle of the road, waving for us to stop. This was a frustratingly routine occurrence in Nigeria, people being stopped and asked for bribes at illegal checkpoints operated by the police and army. Slowing the car, Yemi wound the window down and reached into his pocket. Without even looking at him, he palmed a 20 *naira* note to the soldier who, wordlessly, waved us through and stepped back into the shade. "That isn't oil," Yemi said as we started up again and moved away. "That's our problem."

As we drove north, Yemi reminded me of a story he'd once told me about a venture he'd set up three years earlier with a 50-year-old German friend, a man from Hamburg whom he called Robert.

A successful businessman with a small family, Robert had just gotten divorced in 1995 when he met a female friend of Yemi's who had gone to Germany to study. The two had started dating, and, a couple of years later, once the paperwork was done, they married. Seeking a new life, they decided to move to the Nigerian's home state in southwest Nigeria with a plan to build a business there to provide an income for themselves and, if things went well, jobs for up to 200 people.

After talking to Yemi, who owned several businesses in the area, they sorted out the funding—part of it provided by Yemi—and set up a plant to process soybeans, a crop that could be grown locally and for which there was a ready market. This was in 1999.

Even with Yemi's help, the first year was difficult. There were protracted negotiations to buy the land for the plant and difficulties bringing in machinery that could not be sourced locally. When they test ran the equipment, they found that, of course, the power supply from the state-run grid was off more than it was on, and the generator they'd bought for the plant was too feeble on its own to run the equipment, so they bought another. It was not easy, but at last they were in business.

Then, three months later, the problems started. After they sold their first cartons of soybean oil, a local government official appeared at the factory gate and said that regulations had been broken in setting up the plant. They hadn't, Yemi insisted. They had, the official said, and the council chairman wanted 10 percent of their revenue, paid to a special account, to make the problem go away. Robert refused to pay. He went to the police. The council chairman sent round thugs to smash up his car. The police chief got involved. Not to help, but to demand a cut for himself.

Now Robert understood the problem they faced. Threatened with arrest, Yemi's partner paid up. It meant they were now running at a small loss, but they didn't want to lose the business or let down their workers and the farmers who'd planted soy when they'd heard the factory was being set up. They operated like this for six months and even started to make a small profit. But then the state governor heard what the police chief and head of the local government were taking and announced that he wanted in too.

When Robert again refused to pay, he was arrested for breaking employment laws and bribing officials. Yemi, tipped off, went into hiding. To get himself out of jail, Robert had to pay off the governor, the police chief, the council chairman, and the judge now handling the case. He closed the business and sold the equipment to recoup some of his costs. He and his wife then left for Germany. Yemi used some of his share of what was left to pay off the officials who were still after him. The 200 jobs they had created disappeared with the business. All that remained was an empty warehouse, some unemployed workers, a large pile of soybeans, and a lot of angry farmers.

❧

Corruption in Nigeria is not a story of numbers, even if the numbers themselves are impressive. Since independence, the total stolen or squandered by Nigeria's leaders stands at more than $350 billion, the country's former corruption fighter Nuhu Ribadu said in 2006, and no one since has challenged that figure. But whatever the numbers, even they—extraordinary as they are—do not give a real measure of the problem. The true cost of corruption is added up in the lives ruined and lives lost and the wider damage wrought.

Every year I lived in Nigeria, there was a doctors' strike over unpaid salaries. And every time there was a strike, people died. Bodies would pile up in the morgue as patients went untreated because an official in the ministry had stolen the money needed to pay hospital staff. More than a decade after I arrived in Nigeria, this had still not changed. New strikes take place all the time. Weeks into a dispute in Lagos in 2009, a patient appealed to striking doctors and the government to resolve their issues and get the doctors back to work. "Please, in the interest of the masses, I appeal to doctors and government to end this strike. If they don't, they will cause avoidable deaths," he urged via a newspaper. Dozens died before the dispute was settled.

When it is not doctors, it is teachers who are unpaid. When they strike, pupils suffer. Their education goes on hold and the economy suffers too. Employers in Nigeria routinely lament the dearth of skilled labor. Even failing to clean the streets, when street cleaners are not paid, has a wider cost, a Nigerian friend pointed out. "It is not just about us wanting to live nicely and to have clean streets. Foreign investors are less likely to site businesses in an unattractive city," she said. "So it hurts the economy also."

Great damage is done when the economic choices of officials are distorted by corruption. When corruption flourishes unchecked, money is diverted from vital projects, and bad decisions are made.

When President Obasanjo came to office, he pledged an end to the power cuts that business cites as the biggest obstacle to growth the country faces. Nigeria then produced less than 2,000 megawatts of power on a typical day. A decade later, it still produced under 4,000 megawatts—enough to meet the needs of a medium-sized U.S. city but not those of a country with a population of more than 140 million people and major industry. To meet its needs, Nigeria requires at least 10 or 20 times the power it produces. And the reason it still doesn't get it is corruption. The National Assembly found in 2008 that $10 billion had been spent by Obasanjo on power projects with little to show for it. Some of the money was diverted. Some was just misspent, the assembly reported. It was alleged that bribes were paid by generator makers, among others, to keep power-production levels low.

The effects of this on Nigeria are crippling. In most parts of the country, even those connected to the grid receive power for just a few hours a day. Many more get nothing at all. In most towns, street lights are off more than they are on at night, and when they are off, crime soars. I was nearly killed in the dark of a Lagos street a few months after my arrival, after all. And I was lucky. I got away.

And these power cuts are just one economic problem facing Nigeria because of corruption, which has also distorted import tariffs, exchange controls, and the prices for food and factory inputs, set to suit the needs of officials, not farmers and manufacturers. "In every area of policymaking, decisions are affected every day by bribes paid to officials and ministers: where roads go; who gets what; what things cost. It has a massive impact," the country's leading economist, Pat Utomi, told me one day.

∾

Even before independence, British officials worried about the corruption of those who would soon replace them. They established commissions of inquiry and they jailed those they found guilty of theft and abuse of office. In case after case, my grandfather dealt with officials seeking and accepting bribes or with people impersonating officials to obtain money from businesses. "This sort of extortion is rife," my grandfather wrote after one hearing.

At independence, corruption surged as it did elsewhere when old regimes fell and new ones were yet to be established. Voices rose in protest. Cynically, the fight against theft was used to justify the first coup and others that followed, though the coups did not bring about any changes for the better. Usually, they made things worse.

In the 1970s, when General Gowon was in charge, what best symbolized the corruption of the era was the arrival in Lagos of what was known as the Cement Armada. One month in 1975, officials at the Ministry of Defense ordered 16 million tons of cement, five times more than they needed, and paid more than it was worth too. When the boats they'd chartered arrived, the country's main port was blocked for weeks with hundreds of vessels queuing in the harbor, cement hardening in their hulls as dock workers wondered what to do. While officials enjoyed their giant kickbacks from the suppliers, the port was closed for weeks, and several small firms went bust, unable to get their goods in or out of port.

Though some protested, most Nigerians had long since become inured to corruption, habituated to it. In Achebe's *A Man of the People,* Max, a young, idealistic would-be politician, tried without success to get a crowd to condemn the corruption of his opponents. "As he gave instance after instance of how some of our leaders who were ash-mouthed paupers five years ago had become near-millionaires under our very eyes, many in the audience laughed," the narrator recorded. It was, he said, "the laughter of resignation to misfortune."[1]

With no street protests against corruption, things only got worse.

In the 1980s, with little to hold them back, politicians and officials stole and squandered more than ever before. In the four years a civilian president was in power, ministers inflated contracts and demanded kickbacks and payoffs. Direct theft from the public purse became the norm for those in office. They bought cars and planes and homes abroad. The sums being stolen grew ever larger. When rumors ran around that the authorities were about to stage a crackdown, a series of fires broke out in the headquarters of public buildings. The state-run phone company and the Ministry of Defense went up in flames. The fires were started deliberately to destroy the evidence of the theft. But the rumors were false and no retribution followed.

When the army resumed power on the last day of 1983, hundreds of politicians were arrested for theft. But it soon became clear to most, based on who was detained and who was released, that the arrests were for show and that the detentions were political, not aimed at stamping out corruption at all. After 18 months in office, Muhammadu Buhari was ousted, and Ibrahim Babangida came to power. And once there, Babangida made corruption the virtual purpose of office. When his popularity waned and he needed support, he built a system of government by theft, a kleptocracy, setting up special accounts to siphon off public money to enrich himself and his allies.

It is easy to see the benefits this brought for the elite. Visible from the roads of Minna, a small town 60 miles northwest of Abuja, two houses stand back-to-back, each of them the home of a former president. Babangida owns one. Abdulsalami Abubakar owns the other. The homes are hilltop mansions and are far beyond what a soldier, a government minister, or even the president could normally afford. But money brings power, in Nigeria, and power brings money.

In his eight years in charge, Babangida is thought to have amassed a fortune of billions of dollars. One investigation, in 1994, found $12.4 billion unaccounted for from the Gulf War oil-price windfall that should have accrued to the country in two special, dedicated accounts.[2] In his time in office, following Babangida's departure, Sani Abacha and family are said to have looted more than $4 billion of public funds, and more than $1.3 billion was reported to have passed through London-based banks alone. A decade after starting work, investigators hired by the new Nigerian government in 1999 said they had traced and recovered more than $2 billion of Abacha money, with more expected to be found. During the last few months of Abdulsalami Abubakar's short tenure, following Abacha's demise, the country's foreign currency reserves fell by an unexplained $3.9 billion in just one quarter.

And from heads of state to heads of state-run businesses, from provincial governors to tax collectors, from vehicle inspectors to police inspectors, the list of those who stole is long. But still no one protested.

It was not that every official is dishonest, President Obasanjo said in a sobering speech to the nation on the fortieth anniversary of independence. The problem was that too few people were not, and no one was doing anything about it. "How can anyone deny the blight on our society when we all know how much society has degenerated?" he asked, in the speech broadcast nationwide. "Everyone entrusted with any funds, public or corporate, everyone but a few steals, from paper clips to outright plundering of the nation's resources," the old soldier said. And around the country, few disagreed. They just thought he was one of them too.

∾

Perhaps, I thought, people don't fight fraud because it is everywhere. When I moved to Lagos, I was surprised to see a sign plastered on the walls of a home a few doors down. The owners were away on vacation and had put up a board declaring "BEWARE 419: This House Is Not For Sale."

The number 419 stands for the section of the Nigerian penal code dealing with criminal fraud—and is now used as a synonym for fraud itself. So the sign was a warning to potential dupes not to buy a property that was not in fact on the market. But did that really happen? Was the notice really necessary? I asked Mr. Adebiopon, a man who ran a photocopy business from a stall outside my house.

"The thing is, Mr. Peter, in Nigeria, if you do not stop them, people will sell your house to someone else while you are away on holiday," Adebiopon explained. "Then, when you get back, you get in a fight with the new 'owner,' to decide who really owns your house. So, if you do not want this to happen, you put up this sign. It is like that in Nigeria. It is why no one does business here."

∾

Nigerians, no more naturally honest or dishonest than any other nation, first gained a reputation for fraud and crime in the early years of independence, when a few crime gangs got involved, in a low-level way, in drugs and other trafficking crimes abroad.[3] The country's reputation then imploded in the 1980s, when the next wave of gangs turned to sending out not drugs but faxes and then e-mails to homes and businesses worldwide, seeking to defraud the people who received them.

Typically, today, the sender of the fax, or e-mail, claims to have amassed a large stash of money—usually illicitly obtained—that they need to move abroad. Since the money has not been acquired legally, they need help in getting it out of the country. So, in return for being allowed to use the bank account of the recipient, the sender will give them 10 or 15 percent of the total, a sum they claim would run to hundreds of thousands of dollars or pounds. To get this, all the recipient has to do is either to pay out a small advance fee of a few thousand dollars, to cover the alleged transfer charges, or hand over personal details to their account to allow the sender to make the payment. If they take the former course of action, the recipient will, of course, never hear from the sender again. If they take the latter, their account will be stripped bare a few hours later.

Most people who receive such faxes—or, today, e-mails—recognize them as an obvious attempt at fraud and put them straight into the trash can or junk mail folder. But, if just one in a thousand recipients takes the bait, the whole exercise is worthwhile for the would-be fraudster.

What has grown up since is a loose network of criminal gangs, most based in the southeast but operating across the country. At the lowest level of the operation, the 419 e-mail fraud industry now employs thousands of young and often quite poorly educated Nigerians to spend their days in street-corner Internet cafes writing out standardized e-mails to order. The youths send their mails to addresses provided to them by the people higher up the chain, who are given them, in turn, by the men and women at the top—thought mostly to be either senior officials or businesspeople, or people connected to politicians and the police and protected from arrest and prosecution.

And, with little done to crack down on such crime, this is just one dimension of the fraud industry in Nigeria. Often, the schemes are more elaborate operations. In 2004, a group of Nigerian fraudsters was charged with fraud that almost brought down a bank. The group of three persuaded a senior official of Brazil's Banco Noroeste to transfer $242 million to accounts around the world, for investing in a fictitious scheme to upgrade Nigeria's main airport, on the promise of a personal commission of $10 million. Few such schemes succeed. But all of them, combined with the mountainous e-mail fraud schemes, do great damage to the reputation and economy of Nigeria.

ॐ

Nigerians point out, of course, that corruption is a problem everywhere, not only in Nigeria. This is true. And indeed, since the end of military rule, Nigeria has started a slow and unsteady climb out of the ranks of countries considered the world's most corrupt. Since 1999, when Nigeria was judged the world's most corrupt country by the campaigners Transparency International, the country's corruption ranking has improved, largely due to the efforts of Nuhu Ribadu, the man whom President Obasanjo named as a chair of the new anticorruption body created in 2003, the Economic and Financial Crimes Commission (EFCC).

Despite the pledges made at his inauguration, the anticorruption efforts of Obasanjo's first term were distinctly modest, restrained by his own caution and by political considerations forced on him by the circumstances of his election. Soon after taking office, he sent an anticorruption bill to parliament and ordered the recovery of money stolen by the late Sani Abacha and family. He stopped a series of contracts awarded by his military predecessor, Abdulsalami Abubakar. And he brought in new officials to ensure greater transparency in the running of the Central Bank and big-spending ministries. By most accounts, direct theft from the public coffers dropped. A privatization program that broke the state monopoly on services such as telecoms also cut opportunities for bribe taking and extortion.

But these were easy steps to take. Taking on Abacha's family was not difficult. Since Abacha had passed away in 1998, his family had been left with few political allies. Stopping a few of Abubakar's contracts did not cause a great many problems either. But other former politicians, several former leaders included, were not so easy to hit. They were better protected. In the first four years of Obasanjo's tenure, no prosecutions took place. Progress against corruption was limited.

When Obasanjo was reelected in 2003, things seemed to change. The fight against corruption stepped up a gear. The creation of the EFCC that year made a big difference. Critics, of course, accused its head, the energetic Nuhu Ribadu, of following a political agenda set by the president, pursuing Obasanjo's enemies and letting his supporters off the hook. Ribadu denied the claims and argued that the prosecutions the EFCC launched formed the most sustained fight waged against high-level corruption in Nigeria since independence. And, with over 1,000 investigations and more than 270 convictions under its belt in four years, by 2007 the commission was one of the most trusted bodies in Nigeria.

For the first time since independence, anticorruption officials engaged seriously with their international counterparts, British and American government officials told me. They exchanged information about money laundering and e-mail fraud. In Nigeria, a few big names started to fall. In 2005, it was Tafa Balogun, the head of the Nigerian police, who was found guilty of stealing more than $100 million from police funds. Next, it was former state governors from Plateau State to the Niger Delta who were arrested and charged. James Ibori of Delta State was even charged, among other offenses, with seeking to bribe EFCC officials with a payment of $15 million to drop the case against him.

But, even with such progress, it was clear that there were limits to how far the fight against corruption could go. The sentences passed on those convicted of the most serious crimes of corruption were depressingly light. For a routine robbery, an ordinary Nigerian, if convicted, could face years in prison. But for abuse of high office and the theft of more than $100 million in public funds, the former police chief Balogun got just six months in jail. For his theft of public funds and money laundering, the former Bayelsa governor Alamieyeseigha was sentenced to two years in prison, but was released the next day in exchange for time already spent inside.

And then, in December 2007, seven months after Obasanjo left office, Nuhu Ribadu was forced out of his job by the head of the police, after complaints against him by allies of the new president. The series of cases he was bringing was dropped. Ribadu, who had earned himself many enemies in taking on corruption over the previous four years, was first sent on a training course and then dismissed from the force. He then faced a series of threats that forced him to leave the country. Public confidence in the anticorruption fight of the new government of President Umaru Yar'Adua collapsed at a stroke. When Ribadu's successor, Farida Waziri, was named, few expressed any confidence that the fight would continue. On the initial evidence, they were right not to.

∾

It is clear that no country whose leaders steal or squander $350 billion and distort the economy is going to prosper. And this is what has happened in Nigeria. Corruption has undermined Nigeria's economy since independence. As Nigerians say, the country's experience of corruption is far from unique in the world. It is just more extreme than most.

Born the son of Javanese peasants in a tiny village near Yogyakarta in central Java in 1921, Suharto, the man who was the president of Indonesia for 32 years, was not wealthy by birth. But when he left office in 1998 after more than three decades in power, he was among the richest men in the world. Over his time in office, the president, his wife, and their six children all benefited from corruption, building up huge interests in businesses in the manufacturing, trading, construction, banking, and hotels and tourism sectors. So too did the president's cronies, who saw large parts of the economy parceled out into their hands.

The economic cost of this to Indonesia was serious. When financial crisis struck the Asian region in 1997, the economy of Indonesia shrank by nearly 14 percent in a year, the worst performance in the region. Suharto's "crony capitalism" was widely judged responsible for the speed of the collapse.

But while corruption had indeed undermined the Indonesian economy, the level of corruption remained limited, relative to that of a country such as Nigeria, confined to certain parts of government and certain sectors of the economy. In Indonesia, the relatively controlled corruption of Suharto's regime proved compatible with economic growth because it did not divert the government from policies aimed at growing the economy, wrote the American academic Peter M. Lewis, who has studied the economies of both countries.[4] By contrast, the almost unlimited corruption in Nigeria over the same period bled the country's coffers dry and wrecked its economy, he found.

I explained the contrast to a friend, and he told me a joke some Nigerians tell about the two countries.

A Nigerian and an Indonesian go to London as students in the 1960s and become friends, he said. Forty years pass, and the university invites them back for an alumni meal. Retired and free to travel, they come, and on the night of the reunion, the two old friends meet and, after sharing stories of their student days, invite each other to visit back at home. It is the year 2000.

The first to take up the offer is the Nigerian. He flies to Jakarta and is met at the airport by his friend in a chauffeur-driven limousine. They drive to his friend's home, a mansion on a hilltop with a large swimming pool and a dozen rooms. Impressed, the Nigerian asks his friend how he had amassed his wealth.

"Well," his friend replies, "I was permanent secretary at the Ministry of Works and Housing in Jakarta."

"I hope you don't mind me saying, but it must pay well, to be permanent secretary at the Ministry of Works and Housing in Jakarta," says the Nigerian, with a smile, looking up at his friend's large house.

The Indonesian looks around.

"Don't tell anyone I said this, but do you see that road?" he whispers, pointing toward a highway leading back into the city, full of cars on the busy commute.

And when the Nigerian nods, he taps his chest, and says: "Ten percent."

The next month, it is the Indonesian's turn to visit Nigeria, and he flies to Abuja where he is met at the airport by his old friend, with a fleet of five limousines and police outriders. Driven at speed, they reach the Nigerian's home in the hills outside the city 40 minutes later.

It is an even bigger place, a vast mansion of 40 rooms with three swimming pools, a cinema, and a bowling alley.

Astonished, the Indonesian stands on the terrace and, looking at the Nigerian's house and possessions, says, "You know, when we talked, I never did ask what it was you did for a living."

"Well," says the Nigerian, laughing. "It is funny you ask, but I was permanent secretary at the Ministry of Works and Housing in Abuja."

"I hope you don't mind me saying so," says the Indonesian, "but it must pay very well, to be permanent secretary at the Ministry of Works and Housing in Abuja."

And the Nigerian points to an open expanse of scrub and farmland outside the city where people are trudging on foot, as poor as they ever were. And, in a voice loud enough for all to hear, he roars with laughter and booms: "See that highway there? One hundred percent."

∾

In Nigeria, there is widespread resentment at corruption and the state of the economy. There is anger. But, after decades of living with corruption and its effects, people are now habituated to it. "Nigerians expect to have to use their contacts or to 'settle' an official somewhere along the line, to get anything done," a Nigerian friend told me. "They don't like to have to do it, but they expect it. That is the problem," she said.

This, I thought, was what my friend Yemi had done at the checkpoint on the drive from the delta to Abuja a few years earlier. The money he gave the soldier was handed over without comment, almost without thought, and no anger was expressed. And so, unchecked, corruption flourishes. One hundred percent.

A few years after leaving Nigeria, I heard again from Yemi for the first time in several years. He had left his country, he said, and moved to Germany. He was working now for his former German business partner, Robert, in his old business back in Hamburg and had himself married a German woman.

Yemi had given up on the guest house and a couple of other small businesses he had owned in Port Harcourt. He just could not keep up the fight to keep them running any longer. "In the end, there were too many people to pay. There was too much trouble. Nobody is doing anything about corruption anymore. It's become too hard a struggle," he said.

CHAPTER 12

Divided You Fall

"*Nigerians are too divided*—by tribe, by religion—to unite against our leaders," a journalist friend at Nigeria's *Daily Times* told me as we sat putting the country to rights over lunch in Lagos one day. That's the reason people don't fight the damage done by oil companies and don't fight corruption, he said. "Yes, we are angry and resentful but we are not united. We should come together to pressure our leaders, of course we should. But sometimes," he went on, "it seems we're more at risk of falling apart."

Ever since the country was first founded as two separate protectorates in 1900 and then merged into one 14 years later, people have expressed fears that Nigeria will break apart. Moreover, they have warned, if it does so, the bloodshed and upheaval will be as bad as or worse than when it fought its civil war in the 1960s.

As the country moved toward independence, my grandfather, then chief secretary to the colony, watched in horror as the leaders of the north and south attacked each other in parliament over the Western Region's

---

call to set a date for independence. "I fear the dangers to Nigeria are very real," he wrote at night after watching the Yoruba leader Obafemi Awolowo and the north's leader Ahmadu Bello tear into each other in public.

When the civil war broke out a few years later, it seemed that the country would indeed break up as the east tried to secede. It did not happen. But the country was held together only by the decision of the northern-led army to launch a civil war that cost up to a million lives.

Since then, the divisions between north and south have remained deep. Twenty years after the end of the civil war, it seemed again, in April 1990, that the country might split in two when soldiers opposed to the Babangida regime attempted a coup. They laid siege to army headquarters in Lagos, seized a radio station, and declared the expulsion of five northern states from the federation.

In the end, the coup failed. Babangida reasserted his control. The plotters were caught and executed. But had they succeeded—had the plotters killed Babangida when they tried—the story of Nigeria would have been very different. And still, today, the tensions continue.

∾

To most Nigerians, the fault line that has deepened most alarmingly since independence has been the split between the followers of Islam and Christianity. The growing schism has deepened the political divisions between the more conservative and mostly Muslim north and the more liberal and mainly Christian south.

In the region's long history, this particular divide is a recent phenomenon. Islam itself has been present in the region since the eleventh century A.D., when it became the court religion of the Hausa kings. But, for centuries, few outside the elite subscribed to the Muslim faith. The spiritual needs of the population at large were still met by indigenous religions such as the Ifa faith of the Yoruba and the animist faiths of the northern masses.

And, while over the centuries Islam gradually became more widespread in the north, it did not extend quickly to the south. Wars and rivalries between different states prevented the easy movement of people and faiths. And even when Sheikh Usman dan Fodio's Sokoto Caliphate pushed south into Yoruba territory in the mid-nineteenth century, allying with a local leader to take control of the Yoruba town of Ilorin, the drive south was halted at Osogbo, north of Lagos, in 1834. The main religious divide then was still between Islam and the animist faiths.

When Christian missionaries, many of them former slaves and Christian converts, arrived on the coast in 1841, it was still possible, therefore, for them to introduce Christianity to the south without confronting Islam. And through the second half of the nineteenth century, they managed to spread the new faith across much of the southern half of the country and far up into the so-called Middle Belt without great religious bloodshed. The divisions that exist are recent ones.

Since independence, tensions between Christians and Muslims have grown as Nigerians, disillusioned with what the country has become, have turned more than ever to religion for their answers. And, as an ever more important part of their identity, religion has become one of the great issues dividing the country.

"Here in the north, we believe in one God. We know our leaders are not here to help us, but Allah is. It is in Allah we trust," Ja'afar Adam, a teacher at a Koranic school in Kano, told me. It was the same in the south, a Christian friend offered. "Our leaders are not here for us. Only God can provide. It is only God we can believe in," he said. The problem is it was not the same God.

In both north and south, radicals and evangelicals started proselytizing their faiths in the 1970s. In the north, a radical Muslim preacher,

Mohammed Marwa Maitatsine, founded a fundamentalist sect, outside the Muslim mainstream, which clashed repeatedly with the military authorities from the 1970s onward. Among the calls that upset the army were those he made for the creation of an Islamic state. Only when he was killed alongside thousands of his followers in an uprising in Kano did the sect disappear.

In the south, evangelical Christian ministries set up ever larger churches and went on membership drives, much of their funding coming from Baptist churches in the southern United States. Whipping up religious feeling, they promised adherents a blend of heavenly salvation and earthly reward. And they pledged to defend the Christian faithful wherever they felt their faith was threatened in Nigeria.

In 1999, the banker-turned-politician Ahmed Sani heard the calls from the Muslim faithful for the introduction, or reintroduction, to the north of Islamic law (shariah), once enshrined in practice by the Sokoto Caliphate but set aside by the British and subsequent army regimes. He campaigned for election as state governor that year on a promise to introduce the shariah to his Zamfara State and won a surprise victory as a result. And, within months, the Islamic law code had been introduced to 12 of the 19 northern states by state governors, succumbing to pressure from their voters for a law code they believed would work and be fair for all.

Though it was not the intent, the spread of Islamic law through the north alarmed the Christian minority. It brought clashes both in the north and in the central Middle-Belt region, where the Muslim and Christian communities meet and neither religion dominates. For several years, crises erupted wherever the Christian communities feared their Muslim friends and neighbors were seeking to bring in the shariah, fearing it would be imposed on them, or where Islamic communities felt the shariah was theatened.

∾

The first fighting I saw in person erupted in February 2000 when a march by Christians opposed to Islamic law in Kaduna led to violence. Skirmishes between rival Christian and Muslim gangs led to serious fighting. Buildings were set on fire. People were attacked and killed in their homes.

Hearing the reports, I joined two journalist colleagues, flew north, and hired a car the next morning. As we approached the city's outskirts, our driver, Emmanuel, tore two leafy green branches from a tree on the roadside to drape over the car's hood and trunk, a gesture in Nigeria meant to show that you mean no harm. And then, our car draped in green, we headed for the center. Across the city of 1 to 2 million people, smoke was rising and barricades had sprung up to protect homes and shops from the mobs patrolling the streets. At each barricade we approached, guns were raised, machetes and cudgels held at the ready. We emerged to reassure the defenders we were journalists, unarmed, and made it through.

From the center, we set out again, touring the streets, visiting the hospitals, and talking to community and religious leaders. Heads of both Muslim and Christian communities told us that most of the killings were being done by criminals taking advantage of the protests to loot and steal. The killings were not being done by Christian or Muslim militias, they said. On the streets, we found a different story.

Certainly, the fighting was not purely sectarian. Looting and robbery was widespread. But the killing was being carried out along religious lines. Anyone with a southern-sounding name or accent, anyone with a cross or a Bible, was being dragged out of their home or off the streets in the mainly Muslim, northern parts of the city and killed. And the same was happening to Muslims in the southern parts of town.

Caught trying to escape to safer areas, people would be asked to recite passages of the Bible or the Koran from memory. A slip of the tongue would be fatal. Men would be stripped to see whether they were circumcised and, in a country where most Muslims are and most Christians are not, whether they were or not could be fatal.

When, three days later, the army finally quelled the fighting, medical staff told us that more than 3,000 people had been killed and thousands more wounded. I saw hundreds of bodies in one morgue alone. Tens of thousands of people had fled their homes. An ethnic and religious gulf had opened up in the city as never before.

"I have been here twelve years, but I cannot live here anymore. I have to leave. I have family and they are killing us all," Godwin Nnadiri, a 29-year-old tailor, told me, packing his belongings into his car and joining the heaving queue of traffic heading south once the fighting was over.

"This country, it is falling apart," he said. And so it often seemed.

ᕽ

But, if Christians in the north were fearful of losing their religious freedom, Muslims in the region soon lost faith in their political leaders to implement Islamic law as they felt it should be done.

In towns and villages across the region, alcohol was banned in bars and restaurants, and new laws were introduced regulating relations between the sexes. But the laws were frequently flouted, and little in government itself was changed. Pure Islamic government—justice for all and an end to corruption and misrule—was as distant a hope as ever, and this left many disillusioned. Two dangers emerged out of this. One was a threat to the peace and unity of Nigeria. The other was a threat to lives in the Western world.

Since the overthrow of the Sokoto Caliphate by the British, a radical minority of Muslims has dreamed of creating a new Islamic state in the region. Most Muslims in northern Nigeria still today do not seek an Islamic state. Their version of Islam is a moderate one. But disenchanted by the years of misrule and corruption, and by the half-hearted implementation of the new laws by northern leaders that was meant to end it, growing numbers are giving support to the Islamist cause. New Islamist groups have been formed. And, as has happened elsewhere, this process has increased since the attacks of September 11 on the United States and the subsequent wars waged by the Western powers in Iraq and Afghanistan. Most such groups are still small, but the number of groups and the number of supporters they have are both growing.

In January 2004, a 34-year-old Islamic preacher called Mohammed Yusuf returned to Nigeria from studying in Saudi Arabia. He set up a group called Boko Haram, a Hausa phrase meaning Western Education Is Sinful. Based in Maiduguri, the capital of Borno State in the northeast of the country, the group staged two attacks on police stations in small towns bordering Cameroon in September that year.

Speaking to reporters in 2005, Yusuf claimed the group did not seek violence but said it would fight if it had to against what he called an oppressive and unjust state. He made clear the group's aims and the means it would use if necessary. "I think that an Islamic system of government should be established in Nigeria and, if possible, all over the world," he said. "To do that, we will fight if we have to." Many people dismissed him as a crank at the time. But not so a few years later.

The group skirmished with the authorities from 2006 to 2008. Then, in July 2009, police staged a raid on one of its training camps outside Bama, 50 miles south of Maiduguri. They arrested nine young men and seized several sets of bomb-making equipment. Nine days later, the group responded. As dawn broke over Bauchi, a town 200 miles northeast of Abuja, in the heart of the north, three dozen militants stormed the town's police station, raining bullets down against its dusty walls, shattering its windows, and sending the officers inside diving for cover.

After several minutes of shouts and panic, the police inside recovered their nerve. Grabbing their weapons, they started firing back. A police commander woke the soldiers at the city barracks and called in reinforcements. Soon, a real battle was under way, police and army on one side, militants on the other. Eventually, when the dust settled, it seemed clear which side had won. At least 39 people were dead, most of them militants.

But the following day, the fighting spread to three more northern states: Kano, Yobe, and Borno, and in Borno it lasted four days. The militants had both resolve and strength of numbers, it seemed.

Outgunned by the Islamists, the police in Maiduguri, the capital of Borno, also brought in the army. For four days, plumes of thick black smoke hung above the city as the army opened fire on a mosque, pummeling it and the surrounding homes to which Yusuf and hundreds of his supporters had retreated. Finally the shooting stopped and hospital officials gathered up the corpses. They pronounced more than 800 people dead. Yusuf himself was shot dead by the police after being detained and disarmed by the army.

In Abuja, the government had been alarmed by the uprising. While saying it did not condone the manner of Yusuf's killing, it showed its relief at his death. "What is important is that he has been taken out of the way, to stop him using people to cause mayhem," said Information Minister Dora Akunyili. Police spokesman Emmanuel Ojukwu agreed with her: "This group operates under a charismatic leader. They will have no more inspiration," he said.

But, though Yusuf was dead, few believed that that was the last to be heard from militants in the region. In a country well used to shocks and crises, the uprising had worried many people. Any serious attempt to promote an Islamic state in northern Nigeria would send massive shock waves through the country and threaten the unity of Nigeria, even if it failed. And militant groups were now clearly present in the region and planning attacks. This worried Nigerians. "Nigeria is big enough, and unruly enough already," my friend the *Daily Times* journalist said. "It does not need, in fact it cannot afford, Islamic militants as well."

∾

The West cannot afford Islamic militancy to spread further either. In 2003, al-Qaeda's leader, Osama bin Laden, identified Nigeria's large Muslim population as a good base from which to launch attacks on the West. In 2004, the group Boko Haram staged its first attacks against Nigerian targets. Others followed. And, in August 2009, weeks after the group's July 2009 uprising, the new U.S. secretary of state, Hillary Clinton, visited the country. Washington was concerned that groups apparently linked to, or inspired by, al-Qaeda were seeking a foothold in the country, she told CNN.[1] U.S. counterterrorism officials then revealed that the Nigerian government had, in 2006, laid charges against Yusuf of receiving funding from an al-Qaeda–linked organization, but never brought them to court. And, in September 2009, the Nigerian police paraded for the press an alleged member of Boko Haram, Abdulrasheed Abubakar, who claimed to have been trained in bomb-making in Afghanistan by al-Qaeda–backed groups there.[2]

Then, on Christmas Eve 2009, Umar Farouk Abdulmutallab, the 23-year-old son of a wealthy and well-connected family from Funtua, in northern Nigeria's Katsina State, boarded a plane for Detroit. Flying in from Yemen to Nigeria, to avoid suspicion, he bought a flight from Lagos to Amsterdam and on to Detroit. And, as the plane came in to land in Detroit on Christmas Day morning, as most of his fellow passengers dozed nearby, he sought to detonate a bomb he had earlier concealed in his clothing. Had he succeeded, he would have killed all 290 people aboard and scores more on the ground.

The threat posed by the young Nigerian was already known to some. Two CIA officers at the U.S. embassy in Abuja had been warned in November about his activities by his father, a former minister in the Shagari administration and a senior figure in Nigerian banking. As one of Alhaji Umaru Mutallab's 16 children from two wives, Umar Farouk Abdulmutallab had been brought up with all the privileges afforded to the wealthy elite, of which his father was a prominent member. The main family home in Funtua—one of at least three homes the family owned in the country—was a ten-bedroom mansion with a silver-domed private mosque in the grounds. The boy was educated at an expensive British-run school in Togo, two hours along the coast from Nigeria. And then, already a young man of strong religious beliefs, he attended university in London and become more radicalized still. From there, he headed to Yemen, met more al-Qaeda supporters, and embarked on his al-Qaeda–backed plot to blow up a plane over a U.S. city.

Precisely where he came into contact with his al-Qaeda handlers was not immediately known. But the teacher who had taught him at his British school in Togo said that he had clear extremist views at the time he was in Togo, views he can only have acquired during his earlier upbringing at home in Nigeria. And, in a meeting with State Department officials in Washington in January, Hillary Clinton confirmed that the young man had indeed been radicalized by revulsion at the high level of corruption in Nigeria, and the extreme poverty it created among ordinary Nigerians.

"The information we have on the Christmas Day bomber so far seems to suggest that he was disturbed by his father's wealth and the kind of living conditions that he viewed as not being Islamic enough," she told her officials. And, criticizing the record of past Nigerian governments, she declared: "I do think that Nigeria faces a threat from increasing rad-icalization that needs to be addressed, and not just by military means."[3]

That such a figure should take part in an al-Qaeda bomb plot should, of course, be no great surprise. Bin Laden himself is the son of a wealthy family from an oil-rich state like Nigeria. And, like tens of thousands of other children of the Nigerian elite who travel abroad every year, Ab-dulmutallab had easy access to foreign flights and came from a country that, until the failed Christmas Day attack at least, had not been widely seen as a breeding ground of terrorism. In the days that followed the failed bombing, the attention shown to the Nigerian terror threat changed. Nigeria was placed, for the first time, on a list of 14 countries—a list including Afghanistan, Iran, Libya, Pakistan, Somalia, Sudan, Syria, and Yemen—whose nationals would be required to go through an extra level of security checks, including full-body pat-down searches, before being allowed to fly to the United States.

Such checks can only go so far in eliminating the risk of a bomber getting through the system, the experts cautioned. But the move meant, nevertheless, that the dangers of ignoring Nigeria—and ignoring what has caused the spread of Islamic militancy there—were finally being rec-ognized. This included both the dangers posed to Nigeria—the threats to national unity posed by growing calls for an Islamic state—and the threats posed to the West by thousands more young men like Umar Farouk Abdulmutallab.

∞

The rise of Islamic militancy—and repeated clashes between members of different ethnic as well as different religious groups—has convinced some Nigerians, such as my journalist friend, that Nigerians will never be able to unite around the common cause of fighting corruption and misrule—the twin evils that plague the country and hold back its development.

With the return of civilian rule in 1999, ethnic militant organizations emerged alongside religious ones, arguing, and sometimes fighting, for the rights of the Yoruba, Igbo, and Niger Delta peoples, among others. In a country that is home not only to two world religions but also to more than 400 languages and dialects, alarm grew at the emergence of groups such as a Yoruba nationalist group, the O'odua Peoples Congress, and an Igbo group, the Movement for the Actualization of the Sovereign State of Biafra (MASSOB), an organization that seeks the restoration of Biafra as a state. Such groups risk pushing Nigeria further apart, as was seen in a series of communal massacres involving mainly Christian ethnic Berom farmers and mainly Muslim Hausa cattle herders around the city of Jos in which hundreds died in 2010.

But, though the militants do pose a real threat to Nigeria, they remain a minority in a country where most still strive to live their lives in peace with their neighbors. I saw this reflected on the streets of Nigeria, in the relationships of ordinary Nigerians, day after day and year after year.

I first realized that truth a few months after witnessing fighting on the streets of Kaduna, when I sat on the banks of a river in a forest outside Osogbo, north of Lagos, watching a traditional Yoruba festival. It was August 2000. The festival taking place that day was a celebration of the Yoruba's traditional Ifa faith and of Osun, its goddess of love. From early dawn, thousands came to watch a procession led jointly by an Ifa priest and Osogbo's traditional ruler. At the head of the procession walked a young girl bearing a calabash of sacred offerings. As the crowd looked on, the traditional ruler took the offerings from the calabash and "fed" them to the river where the water coursed through the grove. Finally, the devotees and followers joined in. They walked down to the riverbanks and reached in to sprinkle themselves with the river's holy waters, in a ceremony signifying renewal and rebirth.

Sitting beside me, watching the spectacle, was Mohammed Abdul-wahab, a student of Islamic law from Ogbomosho, an hour or two to the north of Osogbo. Though a Yoruba Muslim, he was married to an Igbo woman, a Christian, and he saw no problem in that, and no contradiction in attending an animist celebration. The Yoruba population may be split, roughly evenly, between Muslims and Christians, he told me, like Nigeria's population as a whole. But this did not mean that they had to fight each other, he said.

"I am a Muslim. My wife is a Christian. But we respect each other's faiths and also those of our Ifa tradition. My faith, Islam, teaches toleration," Abdulwahab told me. So does Yoruba culture, he said. "We Yoruba have a saying that religion is like a house with many doors and windows. There is one faith, but many ways in. What you find, whether your door in is Islam or Ifa or Christianity, it is pretty much the same inside," he explained. "For all those who will go out and fight their Muslim or Christian brothers on the streets, there are many more who will take them into their home to protect them, when fighting breaks out," he added.

What he said was true. While newspaper headlines will often suggest that Nigeria is a country falling apart, the greatest social trend in Nigeria since the civil war ended in 1970 has been toward greater integration in the way people live their lives, the way businesses work, and the way political parties operate together.

I witnessed this one day when I went to watch a soccer match taking place in Surulere, a working-class district of Lagos dominated by the 60,000-seater National Stadium. Joining the crowds pouring into the ground, I made my way up into the stands and took my seat. It was semifinals day in the Africa Cup of Nations. Soccer is the continent's favorite sport, and Nigeria was taking on South Africa for a place in the final.

All around me, tens of thousands of Nigerians, dressed in the green and white colors of the national flag, banged drums, blew trumpets, and chanted for the national team, and it was still two hours to kickoff. If there were any South African fans in the stadium that day, they would have struggled to make their voices heard. When the match ended nearly four hours later, the crowd erupted in celebration. Nigeria had won 2–0. The man who scored both goals was Tijjani Babangida, the son of a Kano family, born and raised in Kaduna. It did not matter to the mostly southern and Christian Lagos crowd that he was a northerner and a Muslim. Nigeria had won, and he was a Nigerian, and that was all.

"You just have to go into a market to see the integration of Nigerians," the country's most eminent historian, J. F. Ade Ajayi, told me some weeks later in Ibadan. "It was not like this forty years ago. Today, you have Hausas, Yorubas, Igbos, everybody together." The economy is "more integrated than ever," he said. "You see intertribal marriages and children growing up in mixed households." There are all sorts of national associations—national student groups, labor unions, church groups, and interfaith groups, he went on. "People might not think it, but people today are less Yoruba or Igbo and more Nigerian. It is happening all over the country."

ᘉ

If Nigeria is more integrated than ever before, Nigerians have, nevertheless, failed since their earliest, precolonial days to unite to put pressure on their rulers. On this I agreed with my journalist friend. This failure is demonstrable in the history of the precolonial states, where misrule was rarely challenged from below, and in that of the colonial era, where pressure was rarely applied on figures such as my grandfather. And it echoes through the past five decades of independence, a story of a people reluctantly, but inevitably, acquiescing to misrule under civilian and military leadership alike.

In a country as disputatious as Nigeria, it is not easy to say why this has been the case. I do not, like my journalist friend, believe that ethnic and religious divides prevent Nigerians from putting pressure on their leaders. This is partly because I don't think the country is as divided as some say, and partly because the history of other countries suggests that ethnic and religious divides need not stop people uniting against unjust rule. "Think of India with its Congress Party campaign against the British. Think of South Africa with the ANC. Think of Indonesia and Malaysia too. They are all ethnically or religiously divided but united against their rulers," I told my friend.

Certainly, Nigeria's independence-era leaders failed to unite the people. In the view of many, they were not real nationalists, but regionalists. Men such as Obafemi Awolowo, Ahmadu Bello, and Nnamdi Azikiwe all talked the nationalist talk when they had to and then, when it suited them, would "retreat into tribe," the writer Chinua Achebe said.[4] As Awolowo admitted in 1960, "the struggles for independence have produced no martyr—no single national hero who is held in reverence and affection by the vast majority of the people of Nigeria . . . a George Washington, a Gandhi or a Nehru."[5] And that has not changed. The Yoruba leader admitted to the playwright Wole Soyinka in 1967 that he always saw himself first and foremost as a leader of his Yoruba people, not of the Nigerian nation. "I've always insisted to myself that my first duty is to the Yoruba nation. We are a nation you know. And I put that nation first, then the one called Nigeria," he said.[6]

But, again, this does not explain the failure to work together for a common cause. The lack of unity is a feature of Nigerian society within ethnic groups too. A Nigerian friend from the south of the country recently returned home after living in Britain for several years. She and her

Nigerian husband bought a plot of land on an up-market development a few miles from my old Lagos home. The location was superb, she said. They bought the land, agreed on the design for their new place, called in the builders, and set to work building their dream home.

The biggest problem was water. With 30 plots and no mains delivery, the area would run dry if everyone dug a borehole, their architect told them. After a survey, they called a resident's meeting, and, addressing his soon-to-be-neighbors, my friend's husband proposed that they collaborate on a common borehole and water system. It would be more efficient for the use of water and would ensure that everyone had enough, he said. They would pay in at the start but it would be cheaper and more reliable in the end. He had barely finished saying this when their neighbors-to-be accused him of being in league with the water company that would maintain the proposed system and of plotting to hold them all to ransom once they had all paid into the scheme. It would not work, they said. He would have to come up with another idea.

Failing to come together, the residents all dug individual boreholes. And, as predicted, this drained the area of water. Now no one gets regular water from the tap. They all have to buy their water in tankers to use for every bath or shower. "It is unbelievably frustrating," my friend said.

The differences of language, culture, and religion may make the country harder to lead. But these differences do not explain the failure to work together. Almost all the residents in the housing development my friend from London told me about were from the same religion and ethnic group: Christian and Igbo, in this case, but they could have been from any other.

At the local level, the failure to work together leads to frustrations such as those suffered by my friend managing a common water supply. At the national level, the failure has helped the country's leaders get away with misrule, corruption, and murder.

CHAPTER 13

Stamp Your Feet

Two Histories of Protest

*T*he man who opened the door of the Abuja hotel room did not look like a rabble-rouser. Peering at me over the rims of his tortoiseshell glasses and adjusting the burgundy cardigan draped over his shoulders, his Honor Justice Chukwudifu Oputa looked every inch the retired Supreme Court justice. But, mild-mannered, law-abiding, and well into retirement though he was, rousing the crowd was exactly what he was trying to do that day—urging Nigerians to stand up to the country's leaders who had been getting away with murder for 50 years.

Born in Oguta, eastern Nigeria, in 1925, Justice Chukwudifu Oputa was already an august figure long before I met him. Starting out as a trial lawyer at 23, he'd been made a judge at 40 and served on the bench for the best part of two decades. When he retired in 1989, he had been a justice of the Supreme Court for the past five years.

When selected by President Obasanjo a decade later to head a commission into human rights abuses under the Abacha regime, he probably seemed a safe pair of hands. He would look at what he was asked to look at and bring no embarrassing facts to light.

From the start, however, Oputa was keen to do more than the minimum required. Along with him on the seven-member panel, he brought together lawyers, human rights advocates, and a prominent Catholic cleric, Father Matthew Kukah. He extended the inquiry's remit back to 1966 to cover the whole period dating back to the first military coup, and not just the Abacha era. And then, when expected to brush things under the carpet, he refused, organizing hearings in public across the country and ensuring they were televised live to a national audience.

"Nigeria is hurting, and the president wants us to be part of the healing process," Oputa told me. The model to be followed was South Africa's post-apartheid Truth and Reconciliation Commission, set up to look into apartheid-era wrongs. Wanting the hearings to expose the truth more than to look for vengeance, the judge sought immunity for witnesses if they provided full answers and made a clear confession. And where he could, he brought perpetrator and victim together to seek reconciliation. "Nigeria has to heal, and for that to happen, the truth needs to get out. The truth needs to be heard," he said.

In sittings lasting more than a year, the panel heard cases that shed light on many of the darkest incidents in Nigeria's long years of suffering under army rule. Time and again, witnesses praised the inquiry as a cathartic experience and a healing process for the nation. But while most of those invited to appear agreed to do so, three former military rulers—the retired generals Buhari, Babangida, and Abubakar—refused to attend, then went to court to suppress the publication of the panel's findings. They claimed that its creation ran against the constitution. The irony of former coup makers appealing to a court to uphold a constitution they had themselves broken was lost on them, it seemed.

Entering the judge's hotel room a few weeks after the hearings concluded, I asked Oputa about the inquiry's investigations of a litany of
shootings, assassinations, rapes, and massacres. The testimony was sobering, he said. I asked him what it had made him feel to listen to so many
hours of such painful accounts.

"What did I feel? It made me angry," the mild-mannered judge
replied, leaning forward in his chair to emphasize his point. "It made me
angry. And not just with the perpetrators but with us, with those who
let it happen too easily."

I wasn't sure I understood. Did he mean angry with Nigerians? I
asked.

"Yes. Angry with Nigerians, angry with myself," he said. "I am
Nigerian. I want things to change. We all do. But we have not made it
happen, and I am angry with Nigerians for that. We have to be more demanding of our rulers," he said.

As the hearings went on, he added, "What I realized is we have not
fought, not really, or not enough. And if you do not fight for your rights
nobody will fight for you. That is my message for Nigerians. If your
leaders steal, if they abuse you, if they abuse your rights, you must shout.
You must complain. Do not accept it. Stamp your feet."

∾

When the Dutch first traveled to Indonesia, it was as traders in the sixteenth century. They followed the Portuguese, setting up scattered trading posts close to markets selling nutmeg, cloves, and peppers, the spice
trade for which the archipelago would soon be famed around the world.
In 1602, the merchants established a company—the Dutch East Indies
Company—to extend their influence in the islands, squeezing out their
Portuguese and British rivals.

In 1800, the operation was taken into government hands when the company fell into financial difficulties. Initially, little changed. Dutch control of the islands remained limited to a thin strip of coast. But the government had plans for its new colony and soon set out to expand the area it ruled.

In Indonesia, unlike in Nigeria, this was not as easy as it appeared. In Java in the 1820s the Dutch encountered fierce revolts. Then, in 1870, when they sought to add the province of Ache to the colony, they faced awesome resistance. And, in the end, the Dutch only took control of the province after a 30-year war that cost the lives of 37,000 soldiers fighting for the Dutch, and more than 100,000 lives in total. Even then, they required a force of 35,000 men to hold their hard-won prize, part of a 70,000-strong force required to maintain their grip on Indonesia as a whole.[1] Not content with a monopoly of the spice trade, the colonial power then claimed control of rubber production and other industries, exacting as heavy a price on the population as the Belgians would later in the Congo. But this control had come at a terrible cost. The comparison of the force the Dutch needed to take control of Indonesia with the 2,000–3,000 men required by the British to take Nigeria—at scant loss of British life—is a striking one indeed.

 relax

Dutch rule of Indonesia at the start of the century was harsh. Punitive raids against those who showed resistance were common. But, even so, resistance grew. In 1920, the Communist Party of Indonesia (PKI) was founded. It was Southeast Asia's first communist movement and, in 1926, it launched an uprising against the Dutch rulers. The uprising was crushed after the Dutch rounded up 18,000 communists and their sympathizers and jailed 4,000 of them. Though defeated, the revolt awoke millions of Indonesians to the injustices they faced. Three movements then emerged—the communist, the nationalist, and the Islamist movements. And, among them, they would shape the future of Indonesia.

When Japan occupied the islands in 1942, the nationalists were the best placed to take advantage of the invasion. Led by a young architect and politician called Sukarno, they had been working hard since the 1930s to build a movement that operated across all ethnic lines. What they needed, and what the Japanese offered, was training in guerilla warfare. With Japanese support, Sukarno built the nationalists into an effective militia, guarding the islands against the return of the Dutch. In return, Sukarno was appointed head of the Japanese puppet administration.

At the same time, the two Islamist movements formed in the 1930s were becoming powerful voices in the countryside. Within a few years, the Association of Religious Scholars and the rival Islamic League would each claim tens of millions of members and come to be seen as the largest, most broadbased anticolonial organizations in Indonesia.

And, first on the ground, the communist PKI party had solid support among the millions of urban poor, and was feared by the Dutch as a powerful force that could help the nationalists challenge Dutch rule in the towns when they returned.

In the end, the war turned and, by 1945, the Japanese were heading for defeat. When the rout became inevitable, the nationalists and their allies rose up against them. Struggling already against the West, the Japanese were soon in retreat. The nationalists, in particular, were now a strong force. So when the Dutch sought to restore their own rule, the nationalists' leader Sukarno declared independence. So-called "struggle committees" were formed across the archipelago to fight the Dutch and, over the next four years, tens of thousands of Indonesians died fighting for independence.

It was, according to historians, one of the largest national revolutions of the twentieth century,[2] and had a profound impact on how the new country would be governed when the Dutch in 1949 accepted their defeat and left. Not all were happy with Sukarno as the new leader. But, for 16 years from 1949 on, Sukarno and the nationalists ruled the archipelago, while the discontent simmered.

∾

The coup that ended Sukarno's rule came on September 30, 1965. A group of Sukarno's leftist allies, known as the 30 September Movement, struck out against those they saw as his enemies. Led by a group of air force officers it managed to kill six of its main targets—all army generals—but failed to finish the job. And, within hours, a countercoup was launched. Days later, a little-known, rightist army general called Suharto had taken power in the army and in the country. It was a position he would hold for 32 years.

Suharto's rule was a bloody one. In his first year in power, his forces slaughtered half a million people in a purge of anyone suspected of sympathies with the leftists around Sukarno. Thousands more were jailed. On the island of Buru, where the country's great novelist Pramoedya Anata Toer was detained for a decade, hundreds of prisoners died from the daily beatings handed out by warders.

But, over those years, the powerful groups formed in the struggle against the Japanese and Dutch—the nationalists, the communists, and the Islamists—still managed to make their voices heard. If the economy faltered, if misrule went too far, they were still ready to take to the streets, their millions of members still ready to confront their wayward ruler.

Over the course of his rule, even while Suharto and his family abused his office to plunder billions, his government therefore brought in technocrats to develop the economy, improve social welfare, and strengthen the country's infrastructure. I would see the result when I visited and compare it in my mind with Nigeria: better roads and more power lines, better schools and more hospitals, a more diversified economy, a literacy rate of nearly 90 percent instead of 60 percent, and an average life expectancy of 70 years, not 45 years.

It was better but not good enough. While the economy grew steadily under Suharto, averaging 7 percent growth over the last two decades, it was still weaker than those of its neighbors. The people demanded more. And, when Asia's financial crisis struck in 1997, and the economy collapsed, popular pressure soon emerged to force the government from office. Students joined with peasants and the city poor to stage protests nationwide. And on May 21, 1998, Suharto was forced from power.

∾

Since independence in Nigeria, no similar uprising has taken place there. There are three main reasons for this and they lie in the country's history, culture, and the habituation of its people to their world in the first decades after independence. Taken together, these factors stifled protests and dampened pressure for change. And, for this reason, Nigerian leaders have felt free to steal billions, run down the economy, and abuse the people. While those in power may have feared the rivals for their job—fellow soldiers or politicians plotting coups—they have never till now feared an uprising of the masses, nor pressure from the business classes against them. And, freed from popular pressure, they have ruled as they pleased.

To understand why, we should start with history. In Nigeria, most early states that formed were autocratic. From Kanem-Borno to Benin, few placed real checks and balances on the actions of their leaders. People deferred to their rulers. The alafin of Oyo was one exception, answering, in theory, to a council of advisers, the Oyo Mesi. The Igbo, among others, had no kings as such and were led by elders. But most states were autocratic and Oyo became more so in its later years. The advent of the slave trade, which empowered the leaders with money and guns, was part of the reason.

Then, in the period leading up to colonial rule, the people who became the Nigerians—living as they were in separate states—failed to
unite to keep out the British. In much of the Niger Delta and across
Yorubaland, local leaders sought the support of the British in conflicts
with their neighbors.[3] In the north, the Hausa emirates refused to help
each other fight Britain's rolling conquest north of the Niger.[4] In the
southeast, the Igbo put up resistance for nearly a decade, different communities banding together in an organization known as the Ekumeku to
keep the British out. But, in most places, the resistance was limited. The
people did not fight to defend their despotic rulers. And the rulers themselves did not unite with each other.

When British rule was established, some protests took place, from
riots against a water tax in Lagos in 1908 to women's protests against a
planned census in the east in 1929. Fifty-five people died in that unrest,
after which the British reorganized the local government system in the
region. But most such protests were limited and localized. When my
grandfather was in Lagos in 1948 and unrest broke out in Accra, he
feared that the rebellion could spread to Nigeria. But it didn't. There
never was a real rebellion under the British regime.

And, five decades on, in 1998, I would see the same thing under the
military. When I arrived, in the last days of military rule, I'd often get calls
from opposition activists, asking me to report on mass protests against the
soldiers. But though I could find almost no one with a good word for the
army, I could rarely, in a country of millions, find more than 200 or 300
people willing to turn out on the streets against them. This was not what
would bring down a government.

And, even ten years later, when president Umaru Yar'Adua refused
to hand over power when out of the country for weeks for health reasons, just a few hundred people turned up to protest in Abuja to press
for Yar'Adua to step down. Demonstrations against corruption and misrule remained rare.

∾

From this long history, what has developed is a culture of power and deference, where rulers rule and fear no rebuke when they do wrong.

As early as 1960, the Yoruba leader Obafemi Awolowo worried that "a public opinion strong and healthy enough to discourage irresponsibility and rascality in public life still has to be developed."[5] And he was right. Even where the theft is openly acknowledged, Nigerians will put little pressure on those responsible. In Chinua Achebe's *A Man of the People,* written in 1966, the crowd, told about the corruption of the country's politicians, thought it could do nothing to stop this happening. "They understood what was being said, they had seen it with their own eyes. But what did anyone expect them to do?" Achebe's narrator asked.[6]

Early in 2002, an accident at a Lagos arms depot killed more than a thousand people, hundreds of them children, drowned in canals around Ikeja as they tried to flee a series of shattering explosions. The government was to blame for the inadequate storage of the munitions that caused the blasts, but did not take responsibility. Talking with colleagues the next day, I expressed outrage. Someone should pay for what they had done, I told my friend Ade Obisesan, a veteran journalist in the bureau. He laughed at the idea and gently mocked me for suggesting it. "That does not happen in Nigeria," he teased. "You know that. But I see that for all I have been teaching, you still don't know your Yoruba sayings," he went on.

"*Agbe fun Oba kii jebi!*—The king can do no wrong! *Ti Oba l'ase!*—The king's word is final!"

In Nigeria, what was once respect for age and authority has become an unhealthy deference. There is a brave minority that challenges the powerful but most people prefer not to. Most of the people I met in the north would defer to authority even when they viewed those who held it with great contempt. In the south, among the Yoruba and others, many I met would prostrate themselves full-length on the floor to greet a person of rank, whatever their opinion of them.

When I arrived in Nigeria, I was horrified to be greeted by Hassan, my new company driver, with the words "Hello, Master." The phrase had colonial overtones, I objected. Couldn't we say something different? My name is Peter, I said. "Can't we use our first names?"

Not really, I was told. Hassan feared that if he got into the habit of being on first-name terms with his boss, he would continue the practice when he went to another employer. And he thought his new boss—Nigerian or foreigner—would not like it. It could cost him his job. So "Mr. Peter" I became.

A few months later, another incident showed me power at play in daily life in Nigeria. One Sunday morning, I got a message from the caretaker of our office building. The previous night, the office cleaners had left a tap open by mistake when the water went off. When the supply returned that morning, water had flooded the office to a depth of several inches. I dashed round to see the damage. When I entered the main room, the cleaners—two women my own age—shrieked and threw themselves full-length in the water at my feet to beg forgiveness and plead for their jobs. I, of course, was horrified.

I raised them to their feet. The flood was not their fault, I protested. Our irregular water supply was to blame, and they knew it. But they did not expect me to be fair and feared for their jobs. Throwing themselves in the water at my feet was their response.

∾

Part of the reason Nigerians have not united historically is that they never had to. The constitution produced in 1947 made the leaders great regional powers. It gave them little reason to cooperate and lots of reasons to compete. And while their counterparts in Indonesia had common enemies to unite against the Nigerians did not. Where the Dutch resisted Indonesian rule, the British handed Nigerians control on a plate.

Generally, the protests against British rule that did take place were peaceful: economic, not political. There were incidents from time to time. Among the worst was a police shooting at a coal mine near Enugu in 1949 that left 21 striking coal miners dead. But, in many ways, the challenges Britain faced at home often seemed greater. The 1930s in Britain was an era of hunger marches, social unrest, and fascists fighting workers on London streets. In Nigeria, relations between the British and ordinary Nigerians were rarely as tense and relations with the elite were generally warm. From the 1940s, traditional rulers were regular visitors to my grandparents' home. From 1952, the Awolowos often came to tea or went for drinks.

When pressure grew to leave—pressure from London and Washington, more than from Lagos or Kaduna—the British went. There were no marches across Nigeria to the sea with a Nigerian Gandhi calling on the British to go. There was no ANC-style campaign asking the British to leave. There was, in short, no national struggle on which to build a unifying, national tale, as there was in Indonesia, India, and elsewhere. Instead, as Awolowo wrote, "there had never been a properly organized countrywide demand for independence which had been spurned or contemptuously turned down by Britain."[7] And since independence, this has cost Nigeria dearly.

Nigeria's government has been seen since independence by most Nigerians not as a government by the people for the people, but as one run by and for a tiny elite. It was not a Nigerian creation and it is not the people's government. In a talk in Lagos in 2009, the playwright Wole Soyinka rued this fact. "A nation is brought into being through the political will of its citizens, not through mere naming," the Nobel laureate said.[8]

Moreover, because most public money comes not from taxes, but from oil sucked up by pipes in the ground, the misuse of its funds seems less egregious to many Nigerians than if it had come from taxes. "The people let the leaders steal the money because they think it is the government's, not theirs," a Nigerian friend told me. "If it came from their taxes, from their sweat, it would be a different thing entirely."

~

Since independence, a few have tried to put pressure on their leaders. In 1950, a former teacher called Aminu Kano formed a party of northern leftist progressives. For more than a decade, his Northern Elements Progressive Union (NEPU) fought for ordinary people and against the elite. In the elections in the 1950s and 1960s, the party won strong support in the northern cities. But, in the countryside, it could not challenge the power of Ahmadu Bello. And it was marginalized during the first years of independence and squeezed out under military rule.

In the 1960s, the people of the east rose in numbers against the massacres carried out in the north and created Biafra. They fought a war and lost, but not for lack of trying. Since then, the people of the delta have resisted the ravages of oil. But more often than not, save in the case of MOSOP, their rebellions have been led by people fighting for their own interests and not for those of the masses. And even MOSOP did not look far beyond the interests of the Ogoni people.

Many others have since emerged on the national stage to challenge those in power. Writers and artists such as Chinua Achebe and Wole Soyinka are prominent among them. Even more fiery and consistent in his criticism of the military regimes was the Afro-beat legend Fela Kuti. Born to a well-known family in the southwest, Fela, as he was always known, earned fame around the country and worldwide in the 1970s and 1980s for his hypnotically powerful music, his wild lifestyle, and his biting critiques of the country's corrupt elite.

Writing most of his songs in pidgin, the vernacular of the Lagos street, Fela spoke out against continued army rule and for the interests of the ordinary man and woman. He demanded that government provide the people with the basic necessities of life: water, food, shelter, and security. He criticized the revolving-door system of power that brought the same military officers and their allies into government, time after time, without any improvement in the lives of Nigerians at all. And when army rule was ending in 1979, Fela sought to run for president as a candidate of his own party, known as the Movement of the People. But nervous authorities, led by the then military ruler General Obasanjo, banned the party and refused to put his name on the ballot. Millions danced and sang to his songs. That made life better but things didn't change.

∾

When I arrived in Nigeria in 1998, there was a prodemocracy movement fighting military rule. The National Democratic Coalition (NADECO) was an alliance of old "prodemocracy" politicians opposed to Abacha. Anthony Enahoro, the man watched by my grandfather calling for independence in 1953, was a prominent supporter. The group was a favorite of the embassies. Other civil rights groups supported its calls. But, try as it might, it failed time and again to bring any mass support out onto the streets.

Where are the masses? I asked a friend from NADECO, after being urged to report a rally that only 50 protestors attended. Too often these were reported as if thousands had attended.

"They are struggling," he said. Really? I asked. "Yes," he said, "but not for democracy," he ruefully admitted.

"For most people," he said, "it's a struggle to get by. That's what they're doing, not our struggle for renewal and change."

"They support us," he added. But, facing the challenges of daily life in Nigeria, people are often too busy getting by, at home or at work, to think about protesting. They are tired out. They are exhausted. They are "managing," as friends would say.

And then, worn down, people get used to how things are. They get habituated. As a foreigner, where I'd see chaos and abuse, Nigerians would see normal life, my friend told me. "If people don't travel, don't see what life should be like, they accept it as how things are. They don't see a reason to get angry at all." Across the continent, people are perhaps too patient, the journalist Richard Dowden, a friend and head of a British think-tank on Africa, wrote. "If Africans fought back sooner against theft and oppression . . . Africa would be a much more peaceful place. Instead, African patience allows exploitation and oppression to thrive until everyone loses their temper and explodes," he said.[9] This is what often happens in Nigeria.

But these things can change. Poor exposure to the media, in the countryside and in the north in particular, is one of the reasons for the accepting attitude of most Nigerians. In Lagos, more than a dozen news-papers are published daily, and it is in Lagos that the pressure on those in power is always greatest. But even there, newspaper sales are tiny. No paper sells more than 40,000 or 50,000 copies daily nationwide, and per-haps half of those are in Lagos. In the countryside and in the north, newspapers are nowhere on the streets.

∾

In Europe, and across the world, mass protests and pressure on leaders have changed history. From England's Peasants' Revolt to the French Revo-lution, emancipation from serfdom was "not granted; it was fought for," according to the political scientist Patrick Chabal. "In the end, subject-hood was abolished by the subjects themselves." That is the difference. That was Europe. "The same did not happen in post-colonial Africa," he said.[10]

Today, however, in many parts of Africa, we can see protest being used to bring change. In the 1980s and 1990s, mass protests by a coalition of blacks, Indians, and others in South Africa helped end white minority rule. And today, protests by the poor of South Africa against corruption have forced even the ANC to push for faster progress in people's lives.

When protests were staged in Nigeria, the leaders cracked down on them. In 1987 and 1989, students and academics led protests against Babangida's economic reforms. The regime took over the student bodies and the universities. When the unions came out on strike against Abacha in 1994, Abacha sent in officials to take them over too.

But, more often, the protest leaders were either co-opted into the regime or failed to gather enough support to make themselves a threat to those in power. Under Obasanjo's civilian regime, the main labor body, the Nigeria Labour Congress, was led by Adams Oshiomhole, a man closely identified with president. When the labor congress could have brought pressure to bear to improve the life of its members, it did not. And, a few years later, Oshiomhole was rewarded with the governorship of his home state.

Even business, which in Indonesia pressured Suharto to run a sound economy, has failed to do so in Nigeria. Foreign business was only interested in oil and allied itself with government. And the leaders of the major Nigerian lobby, the Manufacturers Association of Nigeria, were too often in the government's pockets to press for real change. Rex Oratokhai, a consultant, told me he despaired of the country's business leaders. "Their members have many common interests: steady power supplies, access to finance, and easy business regulation. But their management would not fight for it," he said. The managers of business groups would just use their positions to parlay positions for themselves in government, he said. "It's the first thing I had to learn when I started working with them," Oratokhai told me. "Business organizations in Nigeria are mostly run on the personal agenda of the management, not for the interests of the members. And like that, nothing will change."

CHAPTER 14

Dreams of a New Nigeria

When I arrived in Nigeria, it was a time of hope. The end of military rule was in sight. For me, the journalist, it was an exciting time to come, to witness a moment in history.

But, it was also a time of unease. I knew that my own family's involvement in Nigeria's history was part of the reason that change was needed. Nigeria, like so much of Africa, is as it is in part because of men like Edward Burns, who came, stole land, and imposed their rule. And the coups, the bloodshed, the civil wars, and misrule that followed independence around Africa happened, in part, because of the role of men such as my grandfather: the men who created the new nations unsteady on false foundations and saw them collapse when they left.

But many other things, too, had made Nigeria what it was four decades after independence: the difficulties of forging one nation out of so many peoples, and the ill-timed discovery of oil and the easy riches for those who control it. And, above all, the lack of pressure on the country's rulers to improve life for ordinary people.

And things didn't change as they could. So would they now, 50 years after independence? If Nigeria is to change, who will change it? It will need Nigerians to come together as they never have before. Will it happen? I think it will.

∾

It was late 2009. More than a decade had passed since I first flew into Lagos, arriving to the death throes of military rule. I'd been away awhile. I'd spent three years in Asia and two more in London. Then, late that last year before the fiftieth anniversary of independence, I returned to Nigeria: five decades of freedom and too little change.

I flew first to Abuja, the capital, on a six-hour red-eye flight from London. Then, after staying with friends in Abuja for a day or two, I took a plane to Lagos. Cutting through air heavy with clouds, the plane came in to land. We turned and swung low over the city I'd called home. Friends there had told me it had changed. As we approached, I looked down and saw steam rising from the ground below. It had rained heavily that morning, but now the sun was breaking through. I saw familiar roads, lush green trees, ramshackle buildings, the black lagoon, and the long bridge running its length, linking the city and the islands.

Much looked familiar, but things were not the same, my friends had said. Today, there is not just one small, church-run project to beautify the city—to show the city's potential. There is a whole government project to make it a better city for the people. "You will see it. It is working," my friend had told me when I called.

When we landed, I saw straight away a first sign of what he meant— an improvement for business travelers at least. Instead of scurrying across the tarmac, dodging planes and rainstorms as before, I walked to the terminal directly through a covered gangway. The arrivals lounge was smart and new. Instead of being made to wait for up to an hour for my luggage to arrive, I was able to collect my bags in ten minutes. I was impressed.

Joshua Irabor, a businessman from the delta, heard me comment on the change as he picked up his bags at the carousel. "People who travel know what it is like abroad," he said. "They wanted the same here," he added, before heading for a taxi to the city.

Driving into town, I saw more signs of what my friends had described. It was still Lagos. Shabby and run-down. But in the middle of Airport Road, a line of trees had been planted, brightening up a once-drab area. There were traffic lights, and they were working. When I first arrived in Lagos, there were fewer than half a dozen traffic stops, and they were never on. Now, there were traffic lights, streetlights, and smart new road signs too.

"Are things better in Lagos?" I asked my driver, Ajala, a gravelly voiced character who has seen a lot of the city's toughest times.

"They are. It is true," he answered, his bass baritone scraping the floor of the cab as he spoke. "It is our new governor. He is improving the city for us."

Babatunde Fashola, the new governor, is a lawyer turned politician who took up his new post in 2007. He's made some marked improvements to the city since. Some are the surface things I saw on my way in. "Landscaping and Beautification Project . . . Work of the Lagos State Government," said a panel set up at the side of the road. It was announcing a new park. So this was not a private, church-run garden. The city government was creating them now.

"Security is improving too," Ajala told me as we crossed through Oshodi, passing the spot where I'd almost been killed by armed men a decade earlier. The governor had installed generator units on main roads and connected them to the lights so that when the grid goes down, the lights stay on. Security is better as a result, Ajala explained.

The state was even enforcing traffic laws, he said, as a motorbike taxi rider cut across us at the lights, a crash helmet—an innovation in Lagos—perched perilously high on his head. And there were other, more substantial changes too. The state government was doing a better job of collecting taxes. It was paying its workers on time. There was investment. There were new jobs. People were better off. The state had introduced new, smarter buses. It had plans to build a new bridge, the city's fourth major bridge, to ease the worsening traffic jams. The government was cleaning up garbage dumped around the city.

Was this something done just for the well-heeled parts of town—done for the wealthy residents of the islands? I asked. "Not at all," said Ajala. "This governor, he is good. He is cleaning up the whole city—the islands and the poor parts too." Other friends told the same story.

Lagos was changing, and one friend told me why. Other parts of Nigeria had changed little since I'd been away. In Kano, Ibadan, and the Niger Delta, little had improved since I'd left. Things were changing in Lagos because Lagos people are the most traveled, the best-informed, and the most demanding in Nigeria, my friend said. "It's our attitude," he explained. Lagos is home to the media, and its people see what is happening at home and abroad. "We demand the same." Since I'd left, private TV and radio stations had mushroomed. So had the number of newspapers and the number of people with mobile phones. People were comparing their world with what could be found abroad, and demanding more from the government than before. And that had brought change.

I picked up a copy of the paper left beside me in the car. On the front page, I saw a picture of Governor Fashola. He'd been speaking the previous day at an investment summit for firms from China and Southeast Asia. People around Nigeria should look at what had happened in Africa and Asia since independence, Fashola had told the conference. He'd talked about Lagos and its potential. He'd said it had failed to achieve what it could. Many delegates came from Singapore, a city that had transformed its fortunes in a few short decades. "Look what has happened in Singapore in my lifetime," the governor had said. "It has been done there by people who are not from Mars. So it can be done here."

☙

When Edward Burns arrived in Nigeria a century and a quarter ago, news traveled slowly through the region. Traders on foot were the messengers between towns and cities. Bush wars and conflicts between states had kept people isolated and apart for too long. Britain imposed its rule. In 1908, a mail service was created. Telephones came. But, when I arrived in the country, just a few thousand people were connected at home. There were no cell phones at all. In a country of 130 million, there were under half a million working phone lines. My firm alone owned ten lines, just to have two or three working at any one time. We employed one man, Dauda, full-time just to run daily messages and to plead and wheedle with the state phone company to keep our few lines open.

In 2001, a revolution took place. Within months of coming to power in 1999, Obasanjo had lifted a ban on cell phone companies, put in place by the military. And, in 2000, cell phone operating licenses were sold and networks set up. Within weeks of the first sales, more than 1 million Nigerians had phones of their own. Today, more than 70 million do. Television and radio also grew. The effect has been transforming. Nigerians can talk to Nigerians. The media can reach the people as never before.

∾

Born in Modakeke, on the outskirts of Ife in southwest Nigeria in 1961, Dele Olojede is a Pulitzer Prize–winning journalist. He started out as a reporter at Nigeria's best-known newsmagazine, *Newswatch.* In 1986, a parcel bomb killed the editor, Dele Giwa. It was sent by two men who worked for Babangida. The magazine staged protests but with little effect. No one was reading. Two years later, Olojede moved to America, joining *Newsday* in New York and rising to become foreign editor. In 2005, he won the Pulitzer for his haunting coverage of the tenth anniversary of the Rwandan genocide.

Life in New York was good. But Dele still hankered for Nigeria and the difference he still hoped he could make as a journalist at home. After military rule ended in 1999, he started a slow process of return. In 2007, he moved back for good. The reason he returned was to launch a new media group. The group was called Timbuktu Media. Its newspaper was called *Next.*

In journalistic terms, its goals were not groundbreaking. "Our aim is to put the facts before the people. To arm them with accurate information," he told me in the offices he'd found for the paper in the heart of Lagos Island. As an editor, he wanted scoops, stories, and a mass readership, he said. Don't all journalists? I thought.

What was different, for Nigeria at least, was the means he would use. Newspapers cost a fortune to produce in Nigeria, and distribution is hard. Few papers sell more than 40,000 or 50,000 copies per day. So with no mass readership for the press, the papers have never brought change.

That is why, for Dele, the paper was just a launchpad. "We do not aim to be an ordinary newspaper," he told me, as staff worked busily in the newsroom nearby. "In fact, we don't aim to be a paper at all. We want to be a paper and a platform, a Web site." The idea is to run Twitter feeds and services to cell phones to reach an audience of 25–30 million people, not 25,000–30,000.

"That is the difference. That is what we can do today. It is a reason to be optimistic about change. It is what has changed since I left and it is the reason I returned. Now we have a way to reach out. And we want to reach out however we can, to introduce greater accountability to the system," Dele said.

"We want Nigerians to make the connection between government and their lives. We want to make that connection for people here or in the delta, for example, between the fact that Alamieyeseigha stole all that money and the fact that their son goes to a school with no proper windows. If we do that, then things might change."

∾

Information can save lives. Eighteen months after I arrived in Nigeria, I met a British woman, living in Ibadan, serving with the British-run NGO Voluntary Service Overseas (VSO) as the publications editor of a Nigerian-run charity promoting family health.

As publications editor, Nicola, who would later become my wife, worked on projects from advice leaflets to magazines. The leaflets she produced went to so-called traditional birth attendants, the midwives attending most village births. Few had ever had any formal training. This lack of knowledge helped explain Nigeria's high rate of death in childbirth. The leaflets her group produced provided the sort of knowledge that saves lives. Another problem was the high number of teenage births, ruining many young lives. Nicola started a magazine for school students in the southwest to raise awareness of the risks from early relationships.

The work was important, but often frustrating. "With pamphlets and leaflets, it is difficult to know who we are really reaching, the effect we are having. There are limits to how many people we can reach," she told me one day.

Births and relationships were two concerns. AIDS was another. Though Nigeria had a lower AIDS rate than many African countries, the size of its population alone made AIDS a concern. Not content only to send out leaflets, colleagues at Nicola's NGO and sister organizations went out to truck parks, street corners, marketplaces, and brothels to talk about the dangers. They told prostitutes and their clients of the risks they ran and the high price they could pay, and urged them to protect themselves against AIDS.

One day, I accompanied Lanre Kayode, an activist with one of these groups, on a visit to a Lagos brothel. He arrived with his box of wares: an imitation wooden penis, several packets of condoms, and a set of charts explaining the dangers of AIDS. His routine was good. He gathered the brothel owner and her young workers together and told them what he was doing. He said that he was not there from the government and was not there to shame them. He just wanted to help. He talked about AIDS and other diseases they could contract. He asked them about their practices and whether they insisted their clients use a condom. He asked if they knew how to use them. Most said they didn't.

To much laughter, first one then all the women were shown how to do it on the wooden model. A round of applause followed each time a condom went on correctly. There were ten women working in the brothel, so it took some time.

"The problem today is that our efforts can only reach a few dozen people per day, at best," Lanre told me. "And Nigeria is very big. Lagos alone has many brothels."

Today, though, things have changed. In Abuja, I went to meet a new colleague of Lanre's, working now on the same campaign. "Now it's amazing," she said. "You can send health messages to millions by texting and going online. You can get on private radio. You can send messages and it works."

When the news from Africa is filled with gloom, this is a reason for hope.

∾

For politics to change, people must be able to campaign. New technology, the technology used by Dele Olojede and by health campaigners, can help that happen.

Days after I returned to Nigeria, I went to meet a singer who hopes to use technology this way. Looking carefully at him as he opened the hotel door, I could see the resemblance to his father, Chukwudifu Oputa, that I'd been told to expect. He had the same solid build and hooded eyes. When he spoke, he had the same soft voice too. With more than half a dozen rings and facial piercings, and a line of dreadlocks running halfway down his back, Charles "Charly Boy" Oputa may not dress like the former Supreme Court justice, but appearances can deceive. Both, after all, are campaigners for change.

Now in his fifties, Charly Boy Oputa is a well-established star in Nigeria. When I met him, he had just come down to Lagos to sell his latest album, *Ninja Bike,* to the city's music scene. While we talked, his agent was running through a list of people to be approached to sell the record. Charly Boy wanted promoters and DJs, and the list was just of DJs. "We want someone who will get the message out," he said. The list would have to be changed.

Though we were meeting in a rather shabby hotel in a run-down part of the city, Charly Boy was on a high. A few days earlier, he'd staged a concert for tens of thousands of young people in Abuja—a concert done jointly with a group of churches and youth charities. A TV in the corner was playing a DVD of the event.

Born into a family of lawyers, Oputa got into music at school then fell out with his parents over his plan to have a musical career. Desperate to go his own way, he moved to America to make a life in the business. He was not a success. When he returned, he found fame at home instead.

"I had always wanted to be famous, and now I was. But it was not enough," he told me. He had fame, but not respect. "I found respect in something else. I found it as a social activist."

The campaign he launched in the 1990s was for the rights of tens of thousands of *okada* riders—the motorbike taxis riders who scrape a living ferrying people around the country's towns and cities on motorbikes and scooters. Dodging in and out between cars to get around, they are often knocked off the road by drivers, stopped by the police, and subject to extortion. They are the vital cogs of the country's transport system—able to get anywhere and everywhere fast. And, well-known for his love of motorbikes, Oputa became the champion of their cause.

"Everyone in Nigeria has seen me on TV on my motorbike. They've helped me. I just wanted to return the favor. It sort of grew from there," he said.

Oputa's aim—outside of music—has now broadened to a campaign for the rights of young Nigerians as a whole. His hope is to use new technology to do it. "This country will only change when people, the young people, say 'No. Enough. It is time.' That's my message," he said. "The difference now is how I can do it."

As we spoke, Charly Boy said he and colleagues in the music and film business were building an online database of 2 million names—young Nigerians interested in change. And once it was ready, they planned to organize to campaign on social issues.

Was this really going to happen, I wondered? It has happened around the world. "Why not in Nigeria?" he said. "Nigerians on Facebook now are all talking about how we can change Nigeria, how we can change our situation." Would he make a difference himself? Perhaps not, I thought. He might fail. Bringing change is hard. But even if Dele or Charly Boy and his friends don't succeed, the tools are there for trying. And that's an important change.

∾

The place that seems the most averse to change is parliament, housed in a building that's just a decade old. Reached by an artificial causeway in the heart of Abuja, the National Assembly was finished in 1999. With its white outer walls and mint-green central dome, surrounded by scrub, it stands out proudly against the granite mountain of Aso Rock. And with its sorry record of corruption and shabby politicking, that central dome is the only thing proud about it.

When I first arrived in Nigeria, I would not have met my friend Clement Nwankwo near the Senate building. For several years, under the regimes of Babangida and Abacha, Clement was a wanted man, a thorn in the side of the military.

The first in his family to study law, Clement got into human rights practice after university. It had not been his plan, but fresh from law school, the first practice he was sent to work for was the Legal Aid Council in Ijebu-Ode, a small town a few miles outside Lagos. Starting work there, Clement visited people who'd been detained in prison without trial, some for 10 or 15 years, longer than the maximum sentence they could have received had they faced trial. He set up the first human rights practice soon after.

When elections were held in 1999, Clement headed the country's largest group of election monitors. He was vocal in criticisms of the electoral process. Now, back in Nigeria, I wanted to see him again. I phoned to ask whether we could meet and, if so, where. He said we should meet in his new senate office and my heart sank. Knowing he was working there, I was worried he had somehow sold out. I needn't have worried. "What we need, now, is to bridge the gap between the people outside and the people in here. That is what I am working on. That is why I am here," he laughed when I told him.

∽

Clement's office in the Senate was small, cramped, and windowless. The work was serious: electoral reform. Through his advocacy center in town, he was working with nonprofit groups to get information out about how the electoral and budget processes work, what money there is, and how it is spent in each area. At the same time, he was working with the senate to win them over to electoral reforms.

Two years after the troubled elections of 2007, the government of Umaru Yar'Adua, the new president, announced a constitutional review. The Senate appointed Clement's group to examine the proposals. The crucial changes, he said, were in the setup of the election commission and the way results are announced. Both were at fault in 2007. "Reform of these areas would mark a real change," Clement said. "They would transform the credibility of our elections." The key to getting them passed was persuading assembly members it was in their interest to do so. To do that, he'd built a convincing case.

In meetings with senators, he pointed out that, in the last elections, 80 percent of assembly members had been thrown out by the electorate. When the rule of politics is that anything goes—and that the votes aren't counted—incumbents have no great advantage over anyone else. It's just a rigging contest. If votes cast are counted, and assembly members have served their constituents well, they'd be more likely to stay in office, he argued. They could still play their political games, but serving their people well and counting the votes gave them a better chance of survival. It was in the interests of the members to pass the reforms, he said.

"So did they buy it?" I asked. Clement laughed. "They said so."

By now, we had moved on to Clement's home, a nice but modest flat with a view of central Abuja. Waiting at his door was a local tradesman. He was there, Clement told me, to make a household repair. The catch on his washing machine had broken. The supplier suggested a new machine: the rich man's response but not easy money for most Nigerians. Clement had called in the tradesman to fix the old one. Working in the Senate—where high-spending was the norm—had not corrupted my friend, I was glad to see.

"That place is corrupt," Clement said, pointing out of the window to the Senate. "But it is what we have. So we have to work with it." He was worried by calls from people outside Nigeria for a "revolution" in the country. This was the wrong way to go. It would only mean bloodshed, he said.

"We do need a revolution, but the kind we need is a revolution of people's minds, of their attitude to politics, how they see it, what they do when votes are stolen. We need to make it so that politicians do not feel they can write up whatever result they want and the people will accept it," he said. "We need these reforms. And we need pressure from the people."

So was it happening? "There are good, strong voices, you know, even here in the Senate," he said. "But it is out there that matters." He gestured to the window and the country beyond. "It is what the people are still willing to accept from their leaders. That is what we need to change."

‏‏‎ ‎

The next day I drove to the presidential complex, up the wide, sweeping roads below Aso Rock to the Villa, the seat of the presidency, the center of power in Nigeria. I had been invited by an old friend, Segun Adeniyi, a journalist picked in 2007 as official spokesman of the new president,

Umaru Yar'Adua. As I waited at the gate to pass security, I watched flocks of weaverbirds moving through the trees near the entrance. A gentle breeze was blowing as it often does at the foot of the rock, giving the place a peaceful atmosphere, no hustle and bustle, no roadside sellers, no groaning buses struggling around potholes, no crazy motorbike riders causing mayhem, nothing to remind me I was in Nigeria at all.

Let into the presidency building, I found my way to Segun's office. He came out to meet me. We chatted and I asked what had made him take the role. He'd been reluctant, at first, to give up his job in the media, he said. He was persuaded to do so by his paper's owner, and the new president himself. Yar'Adua, the son of a prominent northern family, had been the choice for president of Olusegun Obasanjo, who saw him, it was said, as a weak figure, unlikely to come after him with indictments on corruption and other charges. And, plagued from the start by poor health, Yar'Adua had, indeed, appeared diffident and indecisive in his first months as president, picking up the nickname Baba Go-Slow for his apparent lack of activity. When his health worsened, gridlock beckoned.

So, what I wanted to know from my friend was whether Yar'Adua was listening, whether he was interested in changing the system. The system had to be changed. Would he do it? What were his priorities?

Segun sat forward in his chair. Numbering them on his fingers, he said the president had three main goals. The first was to bring peace and development to the Niger Delta. The second was to strengthen the national power supply, something that would transform the lives of millions. The third was to provide better infrastructure with new roads and bridges, a change that would boost the economy. "Ask Nigerians. These are the things people want. I read the papers. I see what Nigerians are saying online. And I talk with the president. These are what people want. I tell you, we are listening," Segun said.

This would be good, if it could be believed. Was I right to still be cynical? Later that day, the government would announce plans to pay 10 percent of its oil revenue directly to the delta communities, Segun said. The rebels would announce a cease-fire.

"Peace in the delta is the first step," Segun told me. "Electricity is next. If one thing can transform Nigeria, it is that."

At present, there is not enough power generated to light up a large American city, so Nigerian consumers and industries suffer. The additional capacity to generate electricity lies in underused gas-fired plants in the delta. "So with peace in the delta, we get electricity," Segun said. "What will transform Nigeria is when people, all across the country, can switch on a lightbulb, any time they choose, and see it glow bright. Nobody has done it. That is what the president wants to achieve," he said.

These were nice ideas, I said. But how would the president be held to account if he failed?

"By the people, at the ballot box," Segun said.

I laughed. "The votes will be counted?" I asked.

"Just you watch. We are serious about electoral reforms too," Segun replied, tapping the arm of his chair to make his point. "Not everyone here is serious. It is true. But after what happened last time, the president knows he has to have a credible election next time around. That is why he supports the reforms. Most politicians don't believe he means it yet. But he does. And if we get the reforms, they will need the people's votes. And if that happens, a lot will follow."

∞

A few weeks later, however, just weeks before the end of the year, Yar'Adua boarded a plane for Saudi Arabia to be rushed to a hospital. Long suffering from poor health, his condition had suddenly worsened. For three days, Nigerians learned nothing about the whereabouts of the president, until an announcement that he was in a hospital suffering from pericarditis, a life-threatening inflammation of the lining of the heart.

For two months, government ground to a standstill. In Yar'Adua's absence, no one was in charge. In a country with a long history of military takeovers, the situation was more than troubling.

But in January, a new group formed and called on Yar'Adua either to return or hand over power to his deputy, Goodluck Jonathan. The Save Nigeria Group's campaign was led on the streets by the writer Wole Soyinka, and online by young activists who set up a series of websites to spread their message.

In February, the assembly reacted and declared Jonathan acting president. The next month, Jonathan stamped his mark on the presidency, nominating a new cabinet, and pledged to move ahead on implementing the program of the still ailing Yar'Adua: pushing through electoral reform, ensuring peace and security in the delta, and bolstering electricity generation to revamp the economy. He withdrew charges against anti-corruption boss Nuhu Ribadu, to allow him to return to the country to advise on the corruption campaign.

Encouraged by its apparent success, one of the groups that had campaigned for Jonathan to take over, called on young Nigerians to take to the streets again to demonstrate over issues ranging from corruption to power blackouts. The next week, on March 16, around 2,000 youths demonstrated in Abuja. Organizer Chude Jideonwo told CNN this was "just a first step." "Without social media, we would have been unable to reach the numbers we have so far," he added.[1]

When Yar'Adua finally died, on May 6, 2010, Jonathan was sworn in as president the next day.

To many outside the country, the uncertainty caused by Yar'Adua's collapse was alarming; the sign of a country once more on the verge of breaking apart. To me, the way the situation had been handled—peacefully, with a transfer of power without resort to violence and following popular pressure—was an encouraging sign.

I called my friend Clement Nwankwo. "From what I see, the way it has turned out couldn't have been better for Nigeria," Clement told me, down a crackly telephone line from Abuja. "We have had an unexpected crisis, and we got out of it OK. People got active. It played a major part in persuading politicians to act. Political reform is continuing. There are efforts being made on the delta. The electoral reform bill has been passed. So, who knows, we could have elections in 2011 that are more credible than ever before."

And that matters. The media talk will be about names—about who is running and why, I said. But what really matters—whoever is elected—is whether they feel any real pressure to perform; whether they feel any real pressure to make Nigeria develop as it could.

"A lot depends on what happens in 2011," Clement said. "If people have seen what can be done, there is reason to hope."

The Point
of Departure

hen the boat carrying my grandparents pulled away from the
quay for the last time, they waved to the Nigerian dignitaries and British officials gathered on the harborside and
looked back to the receding shore. It was August 1955. Nearly three
decades had passed since my grandfather had arrived, a fresh-faced youth
in search of adventure; hopeful he could help bring progress to Nigeria.

Ferried across the harbor in a stiff breeze, they climbed aboard the
ship that would take them to England, the *M. V. Aureole.* They drank a
glass of champagne with the governor, who'd come out to see them off.
Then, as the governor returned to shore, they retired to their cabin. Two
weeks later, they sailed in to Liverpool, back in England after almost 30
years away.

And, from that time on, Nigeria was little discussed at home, my
grandmother told me many years later.

They were always interested, she said. They kept up with Nigerian
news and attended talks. They would meet Nigerian friends from time

to time. But it was not their way to look back and wonder what might have been, she told me. "What was the point?" she asked.

By nature an optimist, Hugo had realized by then that a crisis loomed for Nigeria. He thought the British were leaving too soon and had failed. Offered other governorships, Hugo turned them down. The days of colonial rule were over, and he knew it.

His diaries first mentioned his concerns in 1947, the year he worked on the country's first constitution, the one that I believe set Nigeria on the wrong path at independence. The entries are brief, little more than notes, but show how his worries consumed him. He was an outdoors man who liked people and enjoyed getting out. Politics he hated. It was endless talk. "The work is fearful," he would write. "It is wearing and not going well." Observing parliament one day, he wrote, "The atmosphere is terrible, between north and south." Another day, just: "The outlook is bad."

Time and again, he wrote that he sensed failure; both personal and political. "A full morning of the Council of Ministers," he wrote one night. "I came away from it feeling ineffective and depressed." Despite many attempts, he could not get people to work together. Another month, the idea of a week of political meetings filled him with gloom. He feared what would happen when the British left.

To leave Nigeria was a relief. All the while that he was there, he felt the cost to family of his work in Nigeria. The rules of the day at the Colonial Office meant that my grandparents would see little of their children from when my mother was born, in 1937, to their return in 1955. In England it was the norm in those days for those of their class to send their children to boarding school from an early age. But work in Nigeria meant absences far longer than the norm while my grandparents were stationed abroad: anything from nine months to a couple of years, with just short visits home in between.

To an extent that was uncomfortable for all, they became visitors in the lives of their children, who were brought up by relatives, nurses, and nannies. My mother was raised by her aunt and grandmother. She was with them from when she was an infant and felt well-loved. The hard part, she said, was adjusting to visits by parents and siblings she struggled to remember.

When war broke out, and German U-boats patrolled the Atlantic, my grandmother went to South Africa to have her second child, Robert, there. A trip to Europe was too unsafe. When a third child, David, was born in England at the end of the war, my grandfather had to return to Nigeria before the christening. The children's visits to Nigeria, and long holidays in England, made and renewed the natural bonds. But still, it was hard for all concerned.

❧

For all those who venture there today, Nigeria still poses dilemmas more complex than anywhere else I've ever known. It is a place of great hope, great joy, and much laughter, but also one of sadness, suspicion, fear, and pain.

One day at my home in Lagos, the cook who made me meals for four years came to me for help. A gently-spoken man in his fifties, Henri had been losing weight and had gone for tests. The news was bad. He had AIDS and needed help getting drugs. I talked to my office, and between us, we found the money. Antiretrovirals (ARVs) are harsh on the body, and after starting the course he became weak. Soon, he was drifting in and out of consciousness and seemed near death. One day, his 16-year-old daughter, Beatrice, came to see me from neighboring Benin. She wanted to take him home, she told me, to beg forgiveness from the aunt—a declared witch—who she said was killing him with herbs and spells. It was a family quarrel, I was told. The aunt had killed Henri's wife and their youngest child already. If he begged, the aunt would stop her spells. I had to let him return to Benin, his daughter said.

I refused. I knew that Henri had to stay in Lagos. If he stayed, I could keep buying him the drugs that would keep him alive. Taking him home to Benin would kill him, I said.

We argued for hours, and in the end, she gave in. Henri stayed and survived. He recovered his strength. Over the next few years, he kept on working, sending money home to pay for his children to go through school. He built them a new home for when he was gone. But the argument with his daughter troubled me for years.

Why was this my role? What was I doing in Nigeria?

∽

"Enough!" the journalist Dele Olojede exclaimed, laughing, when I told him about my grandfather's role in Nigeria and how it troubled me. "The responsibility for Nigeria today is Nigerians'," he said. "Nigerians need to ask why things are as they are, and not go blaming others. Nigerians need to ask their leaders why Nigeria is as it is, not worry about the past."

For me, understanding what my late cousin and grandfather had done was hard, but necessary. And Nigerians do need to take charge. But they need not act alone. The world needs a strong and healthy Nigeria, not just for the oil, nor just to stop more would-be bombers from striking targets in America. It needs a strong Nigeria for the role it can play in the world.

As it has shown many times since independence, the African giant can be a force for good on the continent. If things go badly wrong in Nigeria, it could sow mayhem across Africa. If they go right, as it could, and should, Nigeria could be a force for good in the world.

There are many things that we in the West can do to help this happen. As individuals, we can press our governments and our companies to help Nigeria and ourselves. It is mainly foreign-owned oil companies that despoil the delta for us to fill up our tanks with Nigerian oil. And the banks that take Nigerian money, the money stolen by the elite, are based in the West.

We can ask our governments to support not their fellow governments but the people of Nigeria and those who hold their leaders to account: the media, the NGOs, the activists and campaigners. These are the people who will bring change. Those in the media, like me, can have a role, working to expose those who pay bribes, the damage done by oil companies, and the banks who hide the governors' money in undeclared accounts.

Since the end of military rule, the sons and daughters of Nigerians who left the country have started to return home from Britain and America. Well-educated and well-connected, they are setting up businesses and calling for change. They are demanding more for Nigeria. The advent of mobile phones and the Internet, the tools of their generation, has made their return easier and mass communication possible. And it is from this emerging class of young professional Nigerians that we can, perhaps, hope most for the push for change to come.

The new tools that Nigerians now have for communication can, of course, be used to divide and to hurt Nigerians, as easily as to change things for the better. This has already happened. But with them, 50 years after independence, Nigeria has a better chance now than ever before to change for the better. Past tolerance of coups is over. Protests are growing. The chance for a new generation to come forward is there. Where and when movements will form to press for change will, of course, be decided by Nigerians, not by outsiders such as me. And that, I think, is something that would have pleased my grandfather. I know it pleases me.

Key Dates in
Nigerian History

37000 B.C.	First proof of human existence in Nigeria: a stone axe left in northeast Nigeria.
9000 B.C.	Late Stone Age evidence of habitation in southwestern Nigeria.
1000 B.C.–A.D. 200	The Nok civilization, whose people created artworks prized today around the world.
A.D. 850	Formation of the Kanem-Borno Empire—one of the first powerful Nigerian states. Formed in northeast Nigeria on the borders of Lake Chad.
A.D. 1000–1400	Foundation of the major Nigerian cities, from the Hausa city-states such as Kano and Zaria in the north to Ife, Oyo, and Benin in the south.
A.D. 1086	The ruler of Kanem-Borno, *Mai* Ibn'Abd al-Jelil, adopts Islam as the state religion, marking the first significant entry of Islam into the north.
A.D. 1450	The start of the Atlantic slave trade. Over the course of 450 years, million of Africans are seized and transported overseas as slaves. The trade devastates communities on the Nigerian coast and inland.
A.D. 1804	Islamic scholar Usman dan Fodio launches an Islamic jihad against the corrupt Hausa kings. He establishes the Sokoto Caliphate, spreading Islamic rule across much of northern Nigeria for the first time.
1807	Britain outlaws the slave trade. London later sends a naval task force to the region to enforce the ban.
1820	Fighting starts between different Yoruba states. The fighting continues, on and off, for 70 years.

1841	A group of former slaves, all converts to Christianity, lands in Badagry, establishing the first Christian missionary presence in the country.
1852	After a battle with British forces, the oba of Lagos agrees to ban the slave trade and grant Britain special trading rights in Lagos.
1861	Britain annexes Lagos, establishing the first colonial presence in the territory.
1875	Businessman Sir George Goldie goes to the Niger Delta to rescue a failing family-owned palm oil firm. He founds a commercial empire there. It establishes the borders of Nigeria.
1885	The Conference of Berlin awards Britain authority over Nigeria, accepting documents presented by Goldie claiming to show local rulers ceding sovereignty.
1900	London declares the creation of the protectorates of north and south Nigeria, taking over control of the country from Goldie's company.
1914	London unifies the two halves of Nigeria as one colony. Frederick Lugard, the former governor of the north, is named governor.
1923	Britain for the first time allows the election of Nigerians to the Lagos Town Council, followed two years later by seats on an advisory council on the running of the colony—the first steps to representation.
1947	A new constitution for the colony grants limited power to Nigerian politicians at the regional and federal level. This constitution is revised in 1952.
1953	Anthony Enahoro, a member of the Yoruba-dominated Action Group, proposes in parliament a vote on a date for self-government. The call speeds up the drive to independence.
October 1, 1960	Nigeria is declared independent from Britain in a ceremony in Lagos. Three years later, it declares itself a republic.
January 15, 1966	A group of young, mainly Igbo, army officers stages the first military coup, killing the prime minister and other northern leaders.
July 29, 1966	A group of northern military officers leads a countercoup. General Yakubu Gowon is appointed the new military ruler.
May 30, 1967	Igbo leader Emeka Ojukwu declares the secession of eastern Nigeria: Biafra. In July, Lagos starts a "police action" to end the secession.
January 15, 1970	Biafra formally surrenders. Up to 1 million people have died in the conflict.

July 29, 1975	Nine years after the coup that brought Gowon to power, he is ousted in a bloodless coup, led by Brigadier Murtala Mohammed.
February 13, 1976	A supporter of Gowon shoots Mohammed dead as he drives through Lagos. His deputy, Olusegun Obasanjo, succeeds him.
October 1, 1979	Obasanjo hands power to Shehu Shagari, a conservative northern politician, elected as president a few weeks earlier.
December 31, 1983	A group of northern military officers leads a coup against Shagari, a few months after disputed elections. Muhammadu Buhari is the new military ruler.
August 27, 1985	In a further coup, Ibrahim Babangida replaces Buhari as military ruler.
June 12, 1993	After nearly eight years in power, Babangida stages elections but then annuls the results after they show Yoruba businessman Moshood Abiola winning.
August 27, 1993	Babangida is forced out of office by fellow officers. He names a southern businessman, Ernest Shonekan, as his interim replacement.
November 17, 1993	Shonekan's defense minister, Sani Abacha, stages the country's sixth successful coup, naming himself president.
June 8, 1998	Military ruler Sani Abacha dies—possibly murdered. His military successor is General Abdulsalami Abubakar.
February 27, 1999	Abubakar stages presidential elections that are won by former military ruler, now civilian, Olusegun Obasanjo.
May 29, 1999	Obasanjo is sworn in as Nigeria's third civilian president.
May 2001	Mobile phone companies start operating in Nigeria.
April 19, 2003	Obasanjo is reelected for a second term.
May 29, 2007	Umaru Yar'Adua is elected Nigeria's fourth president.
November 23, 2009	Suffering from ill-health, Umaru Yar'Adua leaves Nigeria for hospital treatment overseas.
February 9, 2010	The National Assembly names Umaru Yar'Adua's deputy, Goodluck Jonathan, as Acting President, in Yar'Adua's absence due to health.
May 6, 2010	Umaru Yar'Adua dies. Goodluck Jonathan is sworn in as the country's fifth president.

Notes

PROLOGUE

1. See "Leopold's Speech to the Geographical Conference," in P.A. Roeykens, *Leopold II et la Conference geographique de Bruxelles (1876)* (Brussels: Academie Royale des Sciences Coloniales, 1956), pp. 197–99.

CHAPTER 1

1. "Nigeria's New Broom," *The Economist,* June 19, 1999, p, 53.

CHAPTER 2

1. Chinua Achebe, *The Trouble with Nigeria* (Oxford: Heinemann, 1983), p. 1.
2. See also Karl Maier, *This House Has Fallen: Midnight in Nigeria* (New York. Public Affairs, 2000), pp. 185–87.

CHAPTER 3

1. All quotations from Burns come from the memoir, made up of his letters and diary entries, compiled by his parents. A copy is held by the author.
2. This theory of history was also advanced by Professor J. F. Ade Ajayi, Emeritus Professor of History at the University of Ibadan, interviewed by the author in Ibadan in October 2000.
3. See http://www.slavevoyages.org/tast/index.faces, among many other sources.
4. The accuracy of Equiano's account of his life is a matter of academic dispute. Some suggest he was an African American, born in South Carolina. Others suggest that the evidence confirms his story. That the sort of events he recounts took place in their millions is not in any doubt.
5. See *The Life of Olaudah Equiano, or Gustavus Vassa, the African* (New York: Dover Thrift Publications, 1999), p. 31.

6. See Christopher Lloyd, *The Search for the Niger* (London: Collins, 1973), p. 95.
7. Ibid., pp. 137–38.
8. Michael Crowder, *The Story of Nigeria,* 4th ed. (London: Faber & Faber, 1978), p. 54.
9. The modern-day equivalent of the profits was calculated on the basis of average earnings in 1840 and 2005. See http://www.measuringworth.com.
10. Crowder, *The Story of Nigeria,* 75.
11. *The Letters of Queen Victoria, 1837–1861,* published 1907 by A.C. Benson and Viscount Esher, Vol. II, p. 443, quoted in Sir Alan Burns, *History of Nigeria* (London: George Allen & Unwin, 1981), p. 116.
12. According to Sir Alan Burns: "The burning of a native-built town in Nigeria is not as serious a disaster as it sounds. The houses are generally built of mud and the thatched roofs, the only inflammable parts, can be easily repaired." Ibid., p. 126.
13. Quoted in Sanche de Gramont, *The Strong Brown God* (London: Granada, 1975), p. 242.
14. See *Leopold's Speech to the Geographical Conference,* in P.A. Roeykens, *Leopold II et la Conference geographique de Bruxelles (1876)* (Brussels: Academie Royale des Sciences Coloniales, 1956), pp. 197–99.
15. Thomas Pakenham, *The Scramble for Africa* (London: Abacus, 1992), p. 22.
16. Adam Hochschild, *King Leopold's Ghost—A Story of Greed, Terror and Heroism in Colonial Africa* (New York: Mariner Books, 1999), p. 138.
17. Ibid., p. 277.
18. Ibid., p. 3.

<h2>CHAPTER 4</h2>

1. Reverend Samuel Johnson, *The History of the Yorubas* (Lagos, Nigeria: CSS Bookshops, 1921), p. 623. Reprinted in Britain in 1976 by Lowe & Brydon, Printers of Norfolk.
2. Michael Crowder, *The Story of Nigeria* (London: Faber & Faber, 1978), p. 171.
3. Margery Perham, *Lugard, The Years of Adventure* (London: Collins, 1956), p. 62.
4. Ibid., p. 712.
5. Hilaire Belloc, *The Modern Traveller,* in Hilaire Belloc, *Complete Verse* (London. Pimlico Press, 2001), pp. 165–205.
6. Captain Hugh Clapperton's account is quoted in Elspeth Huxley, *Four Guineas—A Journey through West Africa* (London: Chatto and Windus, 1954), pp. 247–48.
7. Crowder, *Story of Nigeria,* p. 182.
8. Ibid., p. 184.
9. Quoted in ibid., p.184.
10. Ibid., p.190.
11. Perham, *Lugard,* p. 647.

CHAPTER 5

1. When my mother complained to her father, years later, that she and her brothers had been brought up by friends and relatives back in England and that he should have chosen a career in Kenya, he explained that he could not have worked in a country where white settlers had come and forced Africans off their land to farm it for themselves. Nigeria was different, he believed.
2. This and all other quotations from my grandfather come from his letters and diaries, copies of which are held by the author.
3. A collection of 14 books of bird paintings by my grandmother, with text by my grandfather, are held at the Nature in Art Museum at Twigworth, near Gloucester, England, and can be seen on request.
4. Obafemi Awolowo, *Awo—The Autobiography of Chief Obafemi Awolowo* (Cambridge: Cambridge University Press, 1960), p. 234.
5. Interview with author in Port Harcourt, November 2001.
6. John N. Paden, *Ahmadu Bello—Sardauna of Sokoto* (Zaria, Nigeria: Hadahuda Publishing, 1986), p. 391.

CHAPTER 6

1. The number of dead in the war is disputed. I use the figure most commonly quoted by impartial sources at the time of up to 1 million dead.
2. For the details of this account, I am indebted to a number of books, including John de St. Jorre, *The Nigerian Civil War* (London: Hodder and Stoughton, 1972), and Olusegun Obasanjo, *Nzeogwu* (Ibadan, Nigeria: Spectrum Books, 1987).
3. Quoted in John de St. Jorre, *The Nigerian Civil War* (London: Hodder and Stoughton, 1972). p. 29.
4. Obasanjo, *Nzeogwu,* pp. 97–99.
5. See the account offered in Ken Saro-Wiwa, *On a Darkling Plain—An Account of the Nigerian Civil War* (Port Harcourt, Nigeria: Saros International Publishers, 1989), p. 17.
6. Ryszard Kapuscinski, *The Shadow of the Sun—My African Life* (New York: Penguin, 2001), p. 103.
7. Ken Saro-Wiwa, *Sozaboy—A Novel in Rotten English* (London: Longman, 1998), p. 181.
8. A. H. M. Kirk-Greene, *Crisis and Conflict in Nigeria 1967–70,* Vol. 2 (Oxford: Oxford University Press, 1971), pp. 451–52.

CHAPTER 7

1. A. H. M. Kirk-Greene, *Crisis and Conflict in Nigeria 1967–70,* Vol. 2 (Oxford: Oxford University Press, 1971), pp. 457–61.

2.   Quoted in Eghosa Osaghae, *Crippled Giant—Nigeria since Independence* (London: C. Hurst & Co., 1998), p. 169.

CHAPTER 8

1.   See Margery Perham, *Lugard—The Years of Adventure* (London: Collins, 1956), p. vi.
2.   Obafemi Awolowo, *Awo—The Autobiography of Chief Obafemi Awolowo* (Cambridge: Cambridge University Press, 1960), p. 308.
3.   Ibid., pp. 314–15.

CHAPTER 10

1.   A 2008 report of the National Oil Spill Detection and Response agency, quoted in Michael Peel, *A Swamp Full of Dollars: Pipelines and Paramilitaries at Nigeria's Oil Frontier* (London: I. B. Tauris, 2009), p. 27.
2.   Human Rights Watch/Africa, *The Price of Oil: Corporate Responsibility and Human Rights Violations in Nigeria's Oil Producing Communities* (New York: Human Rights Watch, 1999), p. 67.
3.   For a detailed account, see Peel, *A Swamp Full of Dollars,* pp. 105–112.
4.   According to the *UN Common Country Assessment on Nigeria,* March 2001, the raid on Odi "resulted in over 1,000 deaths." The exact figures are not known. http://www.ng.undp.org/documents/CCA_2001.pdf (p. 53).
5.   Nicholas Shaxson, *Poisoned Wells: The Dirty Politics of African Oil* (New York: Palgrave Macmillan, 2007), p. 5.

CHAPTER 11

1.   Chinua Achebe, *A Man of the People* (London: Heinemann, 1966), p. 123.
2.   The report was compiled by a committee chaired by the eminent economist Pius Okigbo. It was widely publicized in 1994.
3.   See Stephen Ellis, "West Africa's International Drugs Trade," *African Affairs, Journal of the Royal African Society* 108, no. 431 (April 2009): 171–196.
4.   See Peter M. Lewis, *Growing Apart: Oil, Politics and Economic Change in Indonesia and Nigeria* (Ann Arbor: University of Michigan Press, 2007), p. 7.

CHAPTER 12

1.   "Al Qaeda Could Seek 'Foothold' in Nigeria, Clinton Warns during Trip," CNN, August 12, 2009.
2.   See *"Nigerian 'trained in Afghanistan,'"* at http://news.bbc.co.uk/1/hi/8233 980.stm.
3.   See "Hillary Clinton blames Nigeria leaders for extremism," at http://news.bbc.co.uk/1/hi/8482420.stm.

4. Chinua Achebe, *The Trouble with Nigeria* (Oxford: Heinemann, 1983), p. 5.
5. Obafemi Awolowo, *Awo—The Autobiography of Chief Obafemi Awolowo* (Cambridge: Cambridge University Press, 1960), p. 299.
6. Wole Soyinka, *You Must Set Forth at Dawn* (New York: Random House, 2007), p. 109.

CHAPTER 13

1. Adrian Vickers, *A History of Modern Indonesia* (Cambridge: Cambridge University Press, 2008), p. 13.
2. Ibid., p. 95.
3. Toyin Falola and Matthew M. Heaton, *A History of Nigeria* (Cambridge: Cambridge University Press, 2008), p. 96.
4. Ibid., p. 105.
5. Obafemi Awolowo, *Awo—The Autobiography of Chief Obafemi Awolowo* (Cambridge: Cambridge University Press, 1960), p. 314.
6. Chinua Achebe, *A Man of the People* (Oxford: Heinemann, 1996), p. 124.
7. Awolowo, *Awo*, p. 252.
8. See a copy of the speech in full: http://groups.google.com/group/yorubaaffairs/browse_thread/thread/a1dfb9f4a48f91cb.
9. Richard Dowden, *Africa: Altered States, Ordinary Miracles* (London: Portobello Books, 2009), p. 454.
10. Patrick Chabal, *Africa—The Politics of Suffering and Smiling* (London: Zed Books, 2009), pp. 90–91.

CHAPTER 14

1. See *Rare anger as Nigerian youths hit streets,* at http://www.cnn.com/2010/WORLD/africa/03/16/nigeria.youth.protests/index.html.

A Selected
Bibliography

NIGERIAN FICTION

Achebe, Chinua. *Things Fall Apart*. London: Heinemann, 1958.
———. *No Longer at Ease*. London: Heinemann, 1960.
———. *Arrow of God*. London: Heinemann, 1964.
———. *A Man of the People*. London: Heinemann, 1966.
———. *Anthills of the Savannah*. London: Heinemann, 1987.
Adichie, Chimamanda Ngozi. *Half of a Yellow Sun*. London: Fourth Estate, 2006.
Aluko, T. M. *Chief the Honourable Minister*. London: Heinemann, 1970.
Habila, Helon. *Waiting for an Angel*. London: Penguin, 2002.
Okri, Ben. *The Famished Road*. London: Vintage, 1991.
Saro-Wiwa, Ken. *Sozaboy—A Novel in Rotten English*. London: Longman, 1998.
Soyinka, Wole. *Death and the King's Horseman*. New York: Hill and Wang, 1991.
(And many other works.)
Ulasi, Adaora Lili. *Many Thing You No Understand*. London: Fontana Modern Novels, 1970.

NIGERIAN NONFICTION

Achebe, Chinua. *The Trouble with Nigeria*. Oxford: Heinemann, 1983.
Agbasiere, Sister Joseph-Therese. *Women in Igbo Life and Thought*. London: Routledge, 2000.
Alagoa, Ebiegberi Joe, ed. *The Land and People of Bayelsa State*. Port Harcourt: Onyoma Research Publications, 1999.
Awe, Bolanle, ed. *Nigerian Women in Historical Perspective*. Lagos and Ibadan: Sankore & Bookcraft, 1992.
Awolowo, Obafemi. *Awo—The Autobiography of Chief Obafemi Awolowo*. Cambridge: Cambridge University Press, 1960.
Ben-Amos, Paula Girshick. *The Art of Benin*. London: British Museum Press, 1995.

Boer, Wiebe. "Nation Building Exercise: Sporting Culture and the Rise of Football in Colonial Nigeria," Ph.D. dissertation, Yale University, 2003.

Burns, Sir Alan. *History of Nigeria.* London: George Allen & Unwin, 1981.

Crowder, Michael. *Revolt in Bussa.* London: Faber & Faber, 1973.

————. *The Story of Nigeria.* 4th ed. London: Faber & Faber, 1978.

De Grunne, Bernard. *The Birth of Art in Africa—Nok Statuary in Nigeria.* Paris: Societé Nouvelle Adam Biro, 1999.

De St Jorre, John. *The Nigerian Civil War.* London: Hodder and Stoughton, 1972.

Ellis, Stephen. "West Africa's International Drugs Trade," *African Affairs, Journal of the Royal African Society* 108, no. 431 (April 2009): 171–196.

Falola, Toyin. *Colonialism and Violence in Nigeria.* Bloomington, IN: Indiana University Press, 2009.

Falola, Toyin, and Matthew Heaton. *A History of Nigeria.* Cambridge: Cambridge University Press, 2008.

Human Rights Watch/Africa. *The Price of Oil: Corporate Responsibility and Human Rights Violations in Nigeria's Oil Producing Communities.* New York: Human Rights Watch, 1999.

Huxley, Elspeth. *Four Guineas—A Journey through West Africa.* London: Chatto & Windus, 1954.

Johnson, Reverend Samuel. *The History of the Yorubas.* Lagos: CSS Bookshops, 1921. Rpt. in Britain by Lowe and Brydone Printers of Norfolk, 1976.

Kirk-Greene, A. H. M. *Crisis and Conflict in Nigeria 1967–70.* Oxford: Oxford University Press, 1971.

Kukah, Matthew Hassan. *Religion, Politics & Power in Northern Nigeria.* Ibadan: Spectrum, 1993.

Lloyd, Christopher. *The Search for the Niger.* London: Collins, 1973.

Madauci, Ibrahim, Yahaya Isa, and Bello Daura. *Hausa Customs.* 7th ed. Zaria: Northern Nigerian Publishing Company, 1982.

Maier, Karl. *This House Has Fallen—Midnight in Nigeria.* New York: Public Affairs, 2000.

Morgan, Kemi. *Legends from Yorubaland.* Ibadan: Spectrum, 1999.

Obasanjo, Olusegun. *My Command—An Account of the Nigerian Civil War 1967–70.* Ibadan: Heinemann Educational Books, 1980.

————. *Not My Will.* Ibadan: University Press Ltd., 1990.

————. *Nzeogwu.* Ibadan: Spectrum, 1987.

Ojukwu, Emeka. *Biafra—Selected Speeches with Journals of Events.* London: Perennial Library, Harper & Row, 1969.

Osaghae, Eghosa. *Crippled Giant—Nigeria since Independence.* London: C. Hurst & Co., 1998.

Paden, John. *Ahmadu Bello—Sardauna of Sokoto.* Zaria: Hadahuda Publishing, 1986.

Peel, Michael. *A Swamp Full of Dollars: Pipelines and Paramilitaries at Nigeria's Oil Frontier.* London: I.B. Tauris, 2009.

Perham, Margery. *Lugard, The Years of Adventure.* London: Collins, 1956.

Saro-Wiwa, Ken. *A Month and a Day: A Detention Diary.* London: Penguin, 1995.
———. *On a Darkling Plain—An Account of the Nigerian Civil War.* Port Harcourt: Saros International Publishers, 1989.
Soyinka, Wole. *The Open Sore of a Continent—A Personal Narrative of the Nigerian Crisis.* Oxford: Oxford University Press, 1996.
———. *You Must Set Forth at Dawn.* New York: Random House, 2007.
Suberu, Rotimi T. *Ethnic Minority Conflicts and Governance in Nigeria.* Ibadan: Spectrum, 1996.
UN Common Country Assessment on Nigeria, March 2001. http://www.ng.undp.org/documents/CCA_2001.pdf.
Veal, Michael E. *Fela—The Life and Times of an African Musical Icon.* Philadelphia: Temple University Press, 2000.

GENERAL: NONFICTION

Chabal, Patrick. *Africa—The Politics of Suffering and Smiling.* London: Zed Books, 2009.
Davidson, Basil. *Modern Africa—A Social and Political History.* 3rd ed. London and New York: Longman, 1994.
De Gramont, Sanche. *The Strong Brown God.* London: Granada, 1975.
Dowden, Richard. *Africa: Altered States, Ordinary Miracles.* London: Portobello Books, 2009.
Equiano, Olaudah. *The Life of Olaudah Equiano, or Gustavus Vassa, the African.* New York: Dover Books, 1999.
Fukuyama, Francis. *Trust: Human Nature and the Reconstruction of the Social Order.* New York: Touchstone, 1996.
Hochschild, Adam. *King Leopold's Ghost—A Story of Greed, Terror and Heroism in Colonial Africa.* New York: Mariner Books, 1999.
Iliffe, John. *The African Poor—A History.* Cambridge: Cambridge University Press, 1987.
Ryszard Kapuscinski, *The Shadow of the Sun—My African Life.* London: Penguin, 2001.
Lewis, Peter M. *Growing Apart—Oil, Politics and Economic Change in Indonesia and Nigeria.* Ann Arbor: University of Michigan Press, 2007.
Pakenham, Thomas. *The Scramble for Africa.* London: Abacus, 2001.
Shaxson, Nicholas. *Poisoned Wells: The Dirty Politics of African Oil.* New York: Palgrave Macmillan, 2007.
Thomas, Hugh. *The Slave Trade—The Story of the Atlantic Slave Trade: 1440–1870.* London: Touchstone, 1997.
Vickers, Adrian. *A History of Modern Indonesia.* Cambridge: Cambridge University Press, 2008.

Index

CPSIA information can be obtained
at www.ICGtesting.com
Printed in the USA
LVHW092109100821
694991LV00013B/401/J